Puffin Books

Editor: Kaye Webb

COOKING IS A WAY RC

Have you ever heard of Champ? Do yo
custard? Fay Maschler starts off in Britain and goes on a gastronomic
tour, dividing the book into thirteen sections and encouraging you
to cook some of the delicious specialities of foreign countries. From
Bortsch and Black Forest Cake to Kangaroo Tail Soup, you'll be
staggered by the exotic meals you can produce in your own British
kitchen!

FAY MASCHLER

Cooking is a Way
Round the World

Illustrated by Jonathan Langley

Puffin Books

Puffin Books Penguin Books Ltd,
Harmondsworth, Middlesex, England
Penguin Books, 625 Madison Avenue,
New York, New York 10022, U.S.A.
Penguin Books Australia Ltd, Ringwood,
Victoria, Australia
Penguin Books Canada Ltd, 2801 John Street,
Markham, Ontario, Canada L3R 1B4
Penguin Books (N.Z.) Ltd, 182–190 Wairau Road,
Auckland 10, New Zealand

First published 1978
Published simultaneously in hardback by Kestrel Books

Made and printed in Great Britain by
Fletcher & Son Ltd, Norwich
Set in Monotype Univers Light

Contents

Introduction

The easiest foreign language to learn is food. Pâté risotto spaghetti goulash paella — you're practically fluent already!

Long before people began travelling in any great numbers, traditions of cookery and eating were making conquests and changing habits. The food and spices used for barter and trade spread ideas all over the world.

Climate, history and the culture of any one area have decided to a certain extent its kind of food and the method of preparation. But some cooking combinations are just so obviously delicious that you find them recurring in varied forms in almost all places. Baked Beans as we know them (mostly in tins) may seem forever English, but if you like them — and even if you don't — you will probably relish a French Cassoulet or Mexican Frijoles.

Travelling has brought food here but food can let you travel right in the warmth of your own kitchen. Try some of the dishes of different countries. Speak the language of eating. Food makes friends of us all.

Cooking is a Way Round the World takes for granted that you are familiar with a few basic techniques of cookery like separating an egg, chopping an onion or greasing a baking tin. If you are not, you can always consult *Cooking is a Game You Can Eat,* the Puffin for younger readers and cooks.

However, here are some simple pieces of advice worth remembering:

— Always read the recipe right the way through before beginning to make sure you have all the ingredients, utensils and enough time. To avoid being caught sticky-handed assemble everything you will need before you begin.
— Check if the oven will be needed. If so, turn it on before you start cooking so that it will be at the correct temperature by the time you come to use it. Place the baking dish or tin on the middle shelf of the oven unless the recipe tells you otherwise.
— Wash up as you go along so you are not left with a depressing mountain of dishes at the end.
— Try to do the dishes that require long, slow, cooking

when the oven is being used for something else, so as to save on fuel.
— Make sure that an adult is around for barbecues and campfires.
— Always wear thick oven gloves when taking dishes from the oven, and also when putting them in.
— Remember patience is a kitchen virtue!
— The recipes have been designed to be as authentic as possible, with an eye to availability of ingredients and costs. Stick to them as closely as you can. You will make new discoveries about your taste buds and realize that many so-called foreign foods when mass-produced for shops are but a pale imitation of the real thing.

Some Handy Gadgets

Grater	Colander	Sauce whisk
Egg beater	Rolling pin	Measuring spoons
Sieve	Lemon squeezer	Wooden spoon

Double boiler: If you don't have a double boiler, or one saucepan that sits comfortably in another (without touching the bottom), find a bowl that will. The water in the base saucepan should not reach the level of the bowl or top saucepan.

Measurements and Measuring

Measurements are given in ounces and in grams and sometimes in spoonfuls. If you do not have a set of scales, all the measurements can be worked out in terms of spoonfuls using the table below. A spoonful here means a level one. To make sure you have accurate measurements, heap the spoon with whatever you are measuring and level off with the side of a knife.

1 ounce flour = 25 g = 3 level tablespoons
1 ounce grated cheese = 25 g = 4 level tablespoons
1 ounce butter, margarine or fat = 25 g = 2 level tablespoons
(The 8-ounce rectangular packs are, of course, easy to chop into ounces)
1 ounce currants, raisins, sultanas = 25 g = 2 level tablespoons
1 ounce sugar = 25 g = 2 level tablespoons
1 ounce rice = 25 g = $1\frac{1}{2}$ level tablespoons

When measuring rice in cups use the same cup for the rice and for the liquid and then the proportions will be right, and all the liquid will be absorbed by the grains.

A Note on Ingredients

Supermarkets these days — and shops in general — are getting increasingly adventurous with their range of fruits and vegetables and selection of herbs and spices. However, if you have trouble finding certain ingredients check out your neighbourhood for Greek, Spanish, Indian or West Indian shops, which are often a wonderful (and sometimes cheaper) source of supplies. It is also worth while chatting warmly to a local butcher who might then be willing to chop or bone meat for you or do some other little task that will help.

BRITISH ISLES

Lancashire Hot-Pot
Champ
Oatcakes
Gingerbread
Proper Custard

For such a small island, Britain produces a remarkable range of foodstuffs, many of them of the highest quality. British meat, fish or shellfish is hard to beat, yet too much of it is exported, unappreciated by the natives who spend a relatively small amount of their income on food and eating out. However, it was not always so, and the reputation of English food (sometimes not of the highest) is unfair when you think of how good we are at the sort of meals we enjoy mainly at home : Sunday Lunch, with roast beef and Yorkshire pudding or stuffed roast chicken with bread sauce ; Afternoon Tea with scones, cream and jam and dainty sandwiches, or a High Tea with a delicious spread of hams, cold meat pies, salads, breads, biscuits, cakes and trifles. British food is comforting food. Think of the puddings : steak and kidney, sponge puddings, suet puddings, the last two served with that best of English sauces, a proper custard. It is fun to try the cooking of other nationalities but never forget the virtues of a staunchly British meal !

Lancashire Hot-Pot

Hot-Pot is a comforting dish like a round, fat, jolly person with the welcoming manner typical of the North of England. It's easy to make, and the potatoes that absorb the fat and go crisp on top are a special heaven!

Oven time: 2 hours
Oven setting: electric 325°F, gas No. 3

2 pounds (1 kg) stewing lamb (neck), cut in sections by the butcher
2 onions, peeled and chopped

1 pound (400 g) potatoes, peeled and thinly sliced
A pinch of mixed dried herbs
Salt and pepper
$\frac{3}{4}$ pint (4·5 dl) stock or water

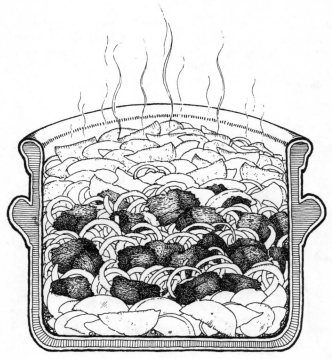

Turn on the oven.

Cover the bottom of an ovenproof dish with a layer of the sliced potatoes. Trim any very obvious lumps of fat from the pieces of lamb. Make layers of meat and chopped onions. Season with a pinch of salt and a sprinkling of pepper. Arrange the rest of the potato slices on top of the meat. Season again with a little more salt and pepper. Make up a beef or chicken stock cube according to the directions on the packet and pour the stock (or water if you have no cube) to come to the top of the potatoes. Cover the dish and put in the oven. Half an hour before the cooking time is up, remove the lid of the dish using your oven gloves and turn up the heat a little to brown the potatoes.

Champ

Although the Irish have suffered in their relationship with potatoes, as in the dreadful famine of 1845–9 when the crop failed completely, they have also thought up some wonderful things to do with them. Like this dish, good enough to eat on its own or with meat or bacon or sausages if you prefer.

1 pound (400 g) potatoes, peeled

About 5 spring onions

¼ pint (1·5 dl) milk

1 ounce (25 g) margarine or butter

Salt and pepper

If the potatoes are of very different shapes cut the larger ones down to size so that they all cook evenly. Put them in a pan of water, add a pinch of salt and bring to the boil. Boil them until they are quite soft. It will take about 20 minutes. During that time peel the outer layers off each spring onion until it is clean and trim the top. Now chop each one into small pieces. Heat the milk in a small saucepan. When the potatoes are cooked, drain them in a sieve, place them back in the pan and mash them with the hot milk (*hot* milk makes them much lighter) and a pinch of salt and pepper. When you have a smooth mixture, add the chopped onions and mix them in. Put the mashed potatoes into a serving dish. With the back of a spoon, make a well in the middle of the potatoes and put in the butter or margarine which will melt. It's much more of a treat this way than mixing the butter in with the milk.

Oatcakes

Oatcakes would provide any good Scotsman or woman with breakfast, dinner, lunch and tea. Just add marmalade, ham, cheese or jam.

Oven time : 20–30 minutes
Oven setting : electric 350°F, gas No. 4

4 ounces (100 g) oatmeal (not instant porridge oats)

A pinch of bicarbonate of soda

1 tablespoon lard

1 tablespoon water

A pinch of salt

In a bowl mix together the oatmeal, the bicarbonate of soda and salt. You can do this with your clean hands. Put the water and the lard in a small saucepan and melt them together on top of the stove. Pour the mixture on to the oatmeal and mix together with a spoon. You should have a soft mixture. If it seems too dry add a little more boiling water from the kettle. Dusting your kitchen surface with oatmeal, roll out the dough until it is thin and then

cut into triangles. Lift these carefully on to a baking tray and cook in the oven until crisp.

Gingerbread

'Gilt on the gingerbread' is an expression that dates from the days when decorated gingerbread was sold at English country fairs. It's still a good tradition to have some nice sticky gingerbread tucked away in the cake tin. This is a simple version and is very good sliced and buttered for tea.

Oven time : 1–1½ hours
Oven setting : electric 325°F, gas No. 3

4 ounces (100 g) self-
  raising flour
A pinch of salt
1 level teaspoon powdered
  ginger
2 ounces (50 g) brown sugar
1 ounce (25 g) oatmeal
3 ounces (75 g) lard

3 ounces (75 g) golden
  syrup
1 teaspoon milk
1 egg
A handful of sultanas or a
  couple of tablespoons of
  apple purée stirred into the
  mixture at the end makes a
  delicious variation

Sieve the flour, salt and ginger into a bowl and mix in the oatmeal
and sugar. Place the lard and syrup in a small saucepan and melt
them together on top of the stove. Add the milk. Mix the liquid
into the dry ingredients. Beat the egg and then mix that in well.
Grease a small loaf tin and pour in the mixture. Using oven gloves
place the tin in the oven.

Proper Custard

One of the best British sauces when not powdered, tinned, or
instant-whipped. You can make pouring custard for lashing over
puddings and fruit, or baked custard which is a dessert on its
own. The secret of custard is not to let it boil. That's called
scrambled eggs.

POURING CUSTARD

1 large egg
A few drops of vanilla
  essence

2 tablespoons white sugar
$\frac{1}{2}$ pint (3 dl) milk

Crack the egg into a bowl and add the sugar. Mix them together
with a whisk. In a saucepan heat the milk until it is very nearly
boiling but not quite. Pour the milk on to the egg mixture and
whisk together. You can now pour all this back into the saucepan
and stir over a very low heat until the mixture thickens, enough
to coat the back of a spoon. Or you can leave the mixture in the
bowl, find a saucepan into which the bowl will fit without
touching the bottom and make a double boiler by putting hot
water into the bottom of the saucepan. Put this whole arrange-
ment on to the stove and stir the mixture in the bowl until it

thickens and coats the back of the mixing spoon. Don't let the water in the saucepan boil.

BAKED CUSTARD

Oven time : 30 minutes
Oven setting : electric 325°F, gas No. 3

Turn on the oven.
Prepare the ingredients in the same way as for pouring custard but put your egg and milk mixture into a small baking dish. Fill a larger shallow dish or roasting pan with about 2 inches (50 mm) of cold water. Place in the oven. Put your dish of custard in the centre of the big dish, making sure the water doesn't slosh over the edge. Find someone to help you remove both dishes from the oven when the custard is firm, and let it cool in its dish surrounded by water. If you like the flavour of nutmeg, a little grated on the top of the custard is delicious.

FRANCE

Poule au Pot
Quiche Lorraine
Cassoulet
Potato Gratin
Crêpes

France and food are two words that seem to go together naturally. French food is too often thought of as posh, rich and hopelessly complicated. In fact some of the best French food is the simplest; the home cooking that every French man and woman spends a good deal of time thinking about, discussing, preparing and digesting! France, because of its size and position, is geographically the ideal land for the production of foodstuffs — a Mediterranean climate in the south and a temperate climate in the north — and still retains its regional variations in food. Local cooking is well defined and lends its name to various dishes — Quiche Lorraine, Salade Niçoise, Potatoes Lyonnaise, to name a few. The recipes in this section do not have elaborate sauces or mysterious flavours (best left to professional chefs or special occasions) : they are examples of the food that cushions family life and turns every French child into a potential gourmet. Any of the meals can be given an extra French accent by following them with a French cheese and some French bread and maybe drinking a drop of wine (watered down of course) as French children do.

Poule au Pot

Henri IV of France had a very fine ambition: that all of his subjects should be able to eat this excellent chicken dish for their lunch on Sundays. It could well explain his great popularity as a king. Try if you can to get a boiling chicken. They are nearly always tastier.

1 chicken
2 onions, peeled
4 carrots, scraped clean
1 leek, well washed and
  trimmed

2 stalks of celery, washed
  and trimmed
6 potatoes, scrubbed clean
  and of even size
Salt and pepper

Stuffing:
4 ounces (100 g) sausage
  meat
1 ounce (25 g) (or a handful)
  of breadcrumbs
1 egg
Salt and pepper

Sauce:
1 egg yolk
2 tablespoons oil
1 dessertspoon vinegar
Salt and pepper

You will need a big saucepan into which the whole chicken fits easily. Make sure the chicken is clean. If in doubt wash it inside and out under the cold-water tap and pat it dry with paper towels. Make the stuffing by putting the sausage meat in a bowl and stirring in the egg, breadcrumbs, salt and pepper, and, if you like, a pinch of dried herbs. When this is well mixed, spoon it into the

chicken, pressing it well back. Put the chicken into the pot with the cleaned vegetables, except the potatoes. Add a big pinch of salt and some pepper. Add enough water to cover the chicken. Bring the panful to the boil on top of the stove and then simmer very, very gently. A small roasting chicken will take about 45 minutes, a bigger one an hour and a real tough old boiling fowl can take up to 3 hours. Half an hour before your chicken will be cooked, add the potatoes. Eat the chicken with the boiled potatoes and with the other vegetables if they are not too limp and overcooked. The water will have turned into a delicious stock and can (and should) be used for soup. To make the sauce : separate the egg. Mix the yolk with the other ingredients and beat with a fork until you have a smooth cream. Serve separately with the chicken and vegetables.

Quiche Lorraine

This egg and bacon tart, which must be one of the most-copied French recipes ever, comes from the part of France close to Germany called Alsace-Lorraine. Although, traditionally, it contains just bacon, eggs and cream, there's nothing to stop you adding cheese, mushrooms, prawns, leeks, spring onions or whatever takes your fancy.

Oven time : 30 minutes
Oven setting : electric 375°F, gas No. 5

Pastry:
4 ounces (100 g) margarine
   or mixture of butter and lard

6 ounces (150 g) plain flour
A pinch of salt
Water

Make this first. Sieve the flour into a bowl, add a pinch of salt. Cut the fat you are using into small chunks and add to the flour. With the tips of your fingers rub the fat and flour together until you get small lumps. Add a tablespoon of very cold water and with as little mixing as possible form the mixture into a ball. You should now have a lump of pastry with a texture that seems like plasticine, i.e. OK for rolling. If it seems too dry and crumbly add a tiny bit more water ; if it's wet and sticky, use a little more flour. Flour a kitchen surface and your rolling pin and roll the pastry out thinly making a roughly circular shape. Place the pastry in a 7- or 8-inch (175- or 200-mm) metal pie dish (metal conducts the

heat better than glass or china), trim round the edges and, if necessary, patch up any spaces or holes.

Filling:

2 thick or 4 thin rashers of bacon
2 eggs
5 ounces (125 g) milk
5 ounces (125 g) (small carton) of single cream
Salt and pepper
1 ounce (25 g) grated cheese (optional)

Chop the bacon into small squares and gently fry them in a small frying-pan. Remove them and put on to the pastry. Beat together the eggs, milk and cream (you can use all milk if you have no cream), salt and pepper and the cheese if you are using it. Pour on to the bacon and, with your oven gloves on, place the tin in the centre of the oven. When it is ready the filling will be firm and golden brown on top. The Quiche may be eaten hot, warm or cold.

Cassoulet

(a cheat)

A true Cassoulet, which the inhabitants of Castelnaudary would tell you comes only from that town, should include preserved goose, lamb, pork and sausages, all of which should wake up as if from a deep sleep in a warm oven in a bed of white haricot beans. Because it is a long and complicated recipe we are going

23

to cheat and do something not quite so good — but much, much better than any tinned baked beans.

Oven time: total $2\frac{1}{4}$ hours
Oven setting: electric 375°F and 325°F, gas No. 5 and No. 3

1 pound (400 g) dried white haricot beans, soaked (see recipe)
$\frac{1}{2}$ pound (200 g) large pork sausages
1 breast of lamb
1 onion

1 bay leaf
1 clove garlic, peeled and crushed
1 small tin of tomatoes
Salt and pepper
A pinch of sugar

An hour or two before you mean to start the Cassoulet, put the beans into a saucepan and cover with cold water. Bring to the boil on the stove, boil for 20 minutes, then take off the heat and leave to stand for at least 1 hour. This saves soaking them overnight. Change the water, add the onion and a bay leaf, bring back to the boil and simmer for 1 hour. (Serious cheats could start here by opening 2 cans of white haricot beans but *not* butter beans.) Half an hour before the beans are ready, turn on the oven to 375°F electricity or gas No. 5. Prick the sausages with a fork. Cut any big lumps of fat off the breast of lamb and divide it into 3 or 4 pieces. Place the meats in a roasting pan and put in the oven for half an hour. Using oven gloves, remove the tin from the oven and lower the temperature to 325°F electricity or gas No. 3.

Place the partly roasted meats in an ovenproof casserole. Add the tomatoes, the garlic and season with salt, pepper and a pinch of sugar. Strain the beans over a large bowl, keeping the water in which they were cooked. Surround the meats with the beans and their onion and pour enough of the cooking water on to nearly cover the contents of the dish. Cover the casserole and cook in the oven for 2 hours. This is a good dish to make when something else is being cooked in the oven at the same time.

Potato Gratin

There are so many things you can do with potatoes that it is a great shame we usually just roast, boil, mash or make chips of them. Cooked in the oven this way with some butter and milk and cheese they are a meal in themselves. You use a shallow dish to get as many crusty top potatoes as possible !

Oven time : 1 hour
Oven setting : electric 325°F, gas No. 3

1 pound (400 g) potatoes, peeled
2 ounces (50 g) butter or margarine
4 ounces (100 g) grated mild cheese
$\frac{1}{4}$ pint (1·5 dl) milk
Salt and pepper

Slice the potatoes carefully into thin rounds (about $\frac{1}{8}$ inch/ 3 mm). With half the butter or margarine grease a shallow oven-proof dish and cover the bottom with a layer of potato slices, cover with a layer of cheese, a layer of potatoes and so on, making the last layer a potato one. Sprinkle with a pinch of salt and two pinches of pepper. Pour on the milk. Dot the top of the potatoes with the rest of the butter. Put in the oven and cook for 1 hour. If the potatoes are not a good golden brown on top turn up the heat to 450°F electricity or gas No. 8 for another 10 minutes.

Crêpes

Crêpe is French for pancake. And like crêpe paper they should be thin and even a little bit wrinkled (just round the edges). You can make these ahead of time and heat them up in a dab of butter in a frying-pan, but it is more fun to let everyone cook their own and eat them on the spot. With a sprinkling of sugar and a squeeze of lemon is the nicest, I think.

4 ounces (100 g) plain flour
A pinch of salt
1 egg
1 dessertspoon cooking oil,
  or melted butter or
  margarine

$\frac{1}{4}$ pint (1·5 dl) milk mixed
with $\frac{1}{4}$ pint (1·5 dl) water
  (the water makes the
  mixture lighter)

Sift the flour and salt into a bowl. With a wooden spoon make a well in the middle of the flour. Break the egg into a cup and pour it into the well. Using the wooden spoon start to stir the egg around and gradually draw in a little of the flour. When the mixture in the middle is thick, add some of the milk and water. Continue stirring from the centre and adding the liquid until finally all the flour has been mixed in and the mixture is the thickness of single cream. It may not take the whole half pint of liquid. Sieve the batter (as it is now called) into a jug. Add the oil or melted butter or margarine and give a stir. It doesn't matter if you don't want to use the batter straight away. In fact some people maintain that it improves with standing. To cook the crêpes, heat a teaspoon of oil in a frying-pan and pour about a tablespoon of the batter into the centre. Tilt the pan until the batter covers the bottom and cook until bubbles begin to appear and the edges turn golden brown. Flip the crêpe over with a fish slice (or toss it if you are daring) and cook for a minute or two. Then start again with the next one.

ITALY

Pizza
Spaghetti
Marinated Oranges

Italian food somehow signifies happiness. It is robust, flavourful and likeable. Spaghetti, pizza and ice-cream are favourite foods and all basically Italian. But don't make the mistake of thinking that's all there is to it. Italy has a long history of fine cooking (think of those Roman banquets) and it was the Florentine cooks that Catherine de Medici took to France with her when she married Henri II of France in 1533, who imparted their skills to the French — a fact that the French don't often mention! Italian cooking is essentially regionalized, and, though modern methods of transport have blurred the boundaries, you will still find more pasta being eaten in the south and more rice and polenta (corn meal) in the north. Question an Italian and you will find that he is really a Roman, or a Tuscan, or a Neapolitan, and he will rave about the food specialities of his region. Oil, garlic and tomatoes are the basis of many sauces and dishes, and if you can use olive oil in the cooking it makes a big difference to the true 'Italianness' of the taste. Also, lash out on a lump of fresh Parmesan cheese. Well wrapped it will keep for ages, and freshly grated Parmesan can turn a dish of plain spaghetti into a real treat.

Pizza

Naples is the town in Italy most famous for pizza and a Pizza Napoletana should be made from bread dough spread with tomatoes, cheese, anchovies, olives and herbs. But there are many other varieties and you could pile on all the things you like best or have lying around (within reason!).

Oven time: 20–30 minutes
Oven setting: electric 450°F, gas No. 8

Pizza Dough (to be made 2½ hours before you want your pizza):

6 ounces (150 g) plain flour	A pinch of salt
2 level teaspoons dried baking yeast	2 dessertspoons cooking oil

Sprinkle the yeast on to a couple of tablespoons of tepid water in a bowl. The water should feel neither hot nor cold when you dip your finger in. Let the yeast dissolve for about 15 minutes. Sift flour and salt into a big bowl. Make a well in the middle of the flour and pour in the yeast mixture. Mix it in roughly. Now add enough tepid water to make a stiff dough. It will probably take between ⅛ pint (0·75 dl) and ¼ pint (1·5 dl). When you have a

firm ball of dough take it out of the bowl and start to knead it on a smooth kitchen surface. With the heel of the palm of your hand push the dough away from you, gather it up and push again. When your arms are aching, or after 5 minutes' kneading, place the dough back in the mixing bowl which you have dusted with a little flour, cover with a clean tea-towel and leave in a warm place (like an airing cupboard or on top of the stove) for the dough to rise and double in size. It should take about 2 hours. After this, slowly mix in the oil, smashing the dough down as you do. When the oil is well kneaded in, shape the dough into three circles on one or two baking trays and leave to 'prove' or rise again, while you make the filling.

Pizza filling:
1 medium tin of tomatoes
A pinch of sugar
A pinch of salt and pepper
1 cooking mozzarella (or 2 ounces [50 g] mild Cheddar cheese)

A few olives or anchovies if you like them
A sprinkling of dried herbs (try oregano)

Strain the tomatoes from the tin and put them into a bowl. Mash roughly with a fork and add the salt, pepper and sugar. Spread the tomato mixture evenly over the pizzas. Cut the cheese into thin slices and lay on top. Add the olives and anchovies if you are using them and sprinkle the herbs all over. Place in the oven. Eat the pizzas while they are still fairly hot.

Some other ideas for fillings:
Lightly fried mushrooms
Slices of sausage

Fried onion rings
Thin rashers of bacon

Spaghetti

Spaghetti is probably the best known *pasta*, the Italian word for all the many shapes of dough which include *vermicelli* (little worms), *farfalloni* (bows), *ditalini* (little thimbles) and many, many more. The trick with spaghetti and all other noodles is not to overcook it but have it *al dente* — still with a little bit of resistance when you bite it. I've heard of people who eat spaghetti with bacon and eggs. This is the really delicious way to do just that and is much quicker to make than Spaghetti Bolognese.

SPAGHETTI CARBONARA

4 ounces (100 g) spaghetti	Salt and pepper
1 teaspoon cooking oil	Some grated cheese
3 rashers of streaky bacon	(preferably Parmesan)
1 egg	
2 tablespoons cream	
(optional)	

Warm a serving dish in a very low oven. Fill a large saucepan with water. Add the oil (it helps stop the spaghetti sticking) and 2 pinches of salt. When the water is boiling add the spaghetti. Very long spaghetti can be pushed in slowly. The bits at the bottom soften and curl round as they get hot. Chop the bacon into small pieces and cook in a small frying-pan until crisp. Break the egg into a bowl, season with a little salt and some pepper, add the cream if you are using it, and beat together. When the spaghetti is ready (try fishing out a strand and biting it after 10 minutes) drain in a colander and tip it into the hot serving dish, which you have taken from the oven using oven gloves. Pour the egg mixture on to the spaghetti and mix it in carefully. The heat of the

spaghetti will cook the egg. Now pour on the bacon pieces and their fat. Mix again and serve with the grated cheese.

Marinated Oranges

Fresh fruit or an ice cream is the usual ending to an Italian meal. This recipe with oranges is more interesting than a mixed-up fruit salad and has just the right refreshing taste after pasta.

4 oranges
4 tablespoons sugar
The grated peel of 1 lemon

The juice of half the same lemon

Peel 3 of the oranges very carefully and scrape off any white pith. Lay each orange on its side and with a small sharp serrated knife slice each one carefully on a large plate (to catch the juice). Place the slices in a bowl and pick out any pips you find. Pour on any juice that has collected in the plate. Grate the lemon peel (just the yellow part, none of the bitter white) and sprinkle on the oranges. Sprinkle on the sugar. Squeeze the fourth orange and half of the lemon you have used for grating. Mix the juices and add to the sliced oranges. Leave in the refrigerator or a cool place for a few hours before serving.

GERMANY and AUSTRO-HUNGARY

Frankfurters with Red
Cabbage and Apples
Goulash
Dumplings
Apple Strudel
Black Forest Cake

The food of these countries represents the down-to-earth virtues of eating. The dishes are, on the whole, straightforward, unpretentious and above all filling ! It is hearty food matched by hearty eaters, who start the day with a good breakfast, and more often than not go on to a second one in the mid-morning. Then after lunch, at that moment round about 4 o'clock when you might feel like a little something, the Germans and Austrians take themselves off to a coffee house to choose one or two or three of their delicious pastries ! The Viennese are particularly famous for their skill as pastry chefs.

Boiled hams, smoked meats, sausages and dumplings of all kinds (so good for sponging up gravy), served with sweet and savoury vegetables like red cabbage and 'heaven and earth' (a combination of puréed potato and apple) feature on the typical German and Austrian menu. Paprika is the clue to Hungarian cooking and Goulash is a worthy national dish, tasting surprisingly different from a stew as we think of it. Try this cookery on a chilly evening, or for a winter Sunday lunch, and you will soon feel its advantages !

Frankfurters with Red Cabbage and Apples

Germany is famous for all kinds of smoked sausages ; *leberwurst, mettwurst, bratwurst, zungenwurst* and so on. The best of the wurst, many people think, are Frankfurters, or Hot Dogs as they have come to be called. The sweet and sour taste of red cabbage and apples goes well with all kinds of sausages, even English ones.

Oven time : 1 hour
Oven setting : electric 350°F, gas No. 4

4 frankfurter sausages
1 large cooking apple
$\frac{1}{2}$ a red cabbage
1 small onion
1 tablespoon wine vinegar

1 dessertspoon brown sugar
1$\frac{1}{2}$ ounces (40 g) butter,
   margarine or dripping
Salt and pepper

Peel any ragged or discoloured leaves off the outside of the red cabbage and slice it as finely as you can. Peel the cooking apple and the onion and chop them both into small pieces. Butter an ovenproof casserole dish with half the butter or other fat. Put in a layer of red cabbage. Sprinkle over it some of the chopped apple

35

and onion, season with salt and pepper and some of the sugar. Repeat this performance until you have used up the ingredients. Add the wine vinegar plus 2 tablespoons water. Dot the top with the rest of the butter or other fat, cover the dish and put it in the oven. When the cabbage is ready you can heat the sausages in a pan of water or you can chop them into inch-length (25 mm) pieces, bury them in the cabbage and return the dish to the oven for another 15 minutes.

Goulash

Gulya is the name for a Hungarian shepherd and *gulyas*, or goulash, might be called Shepherd's Stew. The ingredient that changes a beef stew into goulash is paprika, which, though it sounds hot, is not. It's colourful and enriching and fun to use, but don't go mad! Dumplings (see page 37) would go well with this.

1 pound (400 g) stewing steak
2 onions
2 tablespoons cooking oil
1 level dessertspoon paprika
A pinch of caraway seeds (optional)

1 small tin of tomato purée *or* 1 tablespoon tomato purée from a tube
Beef stock or water
Salt and pepper
1 dessertspoon flour

Chop the stewing steak into cubes of about an inch. Peel and chop the onions. Heat the oil in a saucepan and add the onions. Fry them gently until they soften and then add the meat. When

the meat is beginning to brown add the flour, paprika, salt and pepper and the caraway seeds (if you think you like them). With a wooden spoon stir the ingredients around until they are browned but not burnt. Now add the tomato purée and enough water or stock to just cover the meat (but don't swamp it). Cover the pan and leave to simmer on a low heat for 1½ hours. Or you can transfer the contents of the pan to an oven dish and cook in the oven (especially if it is being used for something else). After the time is up, test to see if the meat is tender and if any more salt or pepper is needed. Soured cream or yogurt is delicious spooned on to this.

Dumplings

If you've ever been called a dumpling, don't be depressed because made this way they can be light and dainty and delicate and delicious – like you! When cooking the dumplings don't keep taking the lid off the pan to look at them. It gets them down. Serve them with stews instead of potatoes or steam them over water and cover them with gravy.

4 ounces (100 g) plain flour
1 level dessertspoon baking powder
A generous pinch of salt
1 ounce (25 g) butter or margarine

1 egg
A little milk
Chopped herbs (optional)

Sieve the flour, salt and baking powder into a large bowl. Cut the butter or margarine into little pieces and rub it into the flour the way you do when you make pastry. Whisk the egg in a small bowl with a fork and add to the flour. (If you want to include herbs –

chopped parsley is nice – mix them with the egg.) Add a little milk until you have a stiff dough. You will not need much. Make little balls with the dough the size of marbles. Now you can either steam the dumplings in a steamer over boiling water or drop them on top of a stew which is nearly ready. Either way cover the pan and leave to simmer for 20 minutes. When you lift the lid the dumplings will be (should be) twice their original size.

Apple Strudel

Making strudel pastry is an art in itself for it should be rolled and stretched until it is so thin you could practically read a newspaper through it. If you live near a Greek bakery you could use their *fila* pastry sold in sheets. Failing that frozen puff pastry rolled as thin as possible will do. Strudel can be made with any fruit – or even a meat filling – but apples and sultanas are the most usual and I think the best.

Oven time : 30 minutes
Oven setting : electric 400°F, gas No. 6

1 packet of frozen puff
  pastry (thawed)
1 pound (400 g) cooking
  apples or dessert apples
2 ounces (50 g) sultanas

1 ounce (25 g) butter
2–3 tablespoons sugar
A pinch of cinnamon
A little milk
A little icing sugar

On a floured board roll out the thawed pastry until you have a rectangle shape as thin as you can make it. Carefully lift (it helps if first you gently, loosely fold it up) the pastry on to a baking tin and spread out. Peel, core and slice the apples. In a bowl mix the slices with the sugar (use 3 tablespoons for cookers, less for dessert apples), the sultanas, the cinnamon and the butter chopped into little pieces. Spread the filling down the centre of the

pastry and fold the sides in to make a parcel. Brush the top with a little milk and place in the oven till the pastry is golden. Remove from the oven using gloves and dust strudel with a little icing sugar before serving.

Black Forest Cake

(*a short cut through*)

In Germany this is a popular treat at tea-time when the Germans drink coffee. It also makes a lovely pudding. It's the combination of chocolate and cherries that is so good. This is a simplified version of the real thing, which traditionally has a pastry base.

Oven time : 25 minutes
Oven setting : electric 325°F, gas No. 3

6 ounces (150 g) self-raising flour	2 eggs
6 ounces (150 g) soft margarine	1 tablespoon cocoa
6 ounces (150 g) castor sugar	A pinch of salt

Turn on the oven. Grease and flour two 7-inch (175-mm) cake tins. There are two ways of making this cake. You can put all the ingredients into a bowl (first mixing the cocoa with a little water) and beat with a wooden spoon or electric beater. Or you can cream together the margarine and sugar, beat in the eggs, followed by the cocoa mixed with a little water, and lastly fold in the flour. This is the more traditional method, but both work well. Divide the mixture between the two tins, spreading the mixture as evenly as possible, and bake in the centre of the oven. When they are done, turn out and cool on a wire rack.

To assemble the Black Forest Cake

1 tin of stoned cherries
2 tablespoons sugar

1 carton of double cream or whipping cream (optional)

Drain the tin of cherries, saving the juice, and put the juice and sugar into a saucepan. Boil this mixture until it thickens and looks syrupy. Pour it over the cherries and leave it to cool. Place one cake layer on a plate and cover with the cherries and their syrup. If you decide to use cream, pour it into a bowl and whip until stiff with an egg beater. Using half of the cream, cover the cherries, then place the other cake layer on top and cover that with the rest of the cream. A little grated chocolate sprinkled on top looks pretty. If you are not using cream, just put the other cake layer straight on to the cherries and maybe sift a little icing sugar on top for decoration.

SPAIN and PORTUGAL

Gazpacho
Paella
Salt Cod
Tortilla
Torrijas

The Moorish occupation of Spain and Portugal had a considerable influence on the food of these countries, not only on the cooking styles but on the ingredients used. The Moors brought with them and cultivated rice (the basis for that most popular dish, Paella), oranges and lemons, and spices like cumin and aniseed that give Spanish cooking its slightly Eastern flavour. The Moors also planted groves of almond trees and these nuts, both plain and sweetened, are widely used in Spanish food. Sugared almonds, I think you will agree, are very morish!

Spanish cooking does not rely on sauces or any complicated processes. The ingredients, though often inventively mixed — as in the Spanish stews of different meats, sausages and dried and fresh vegetables (*cocido*) — always taste of themselves. In the poorer areas of Spain and Portugal, the produce that is available is used ingeniously. There are as many ways, it is said, of preparing salt cod (*bacalhau*) as there are days in the year. Spanish olive oil is quite strongly flavoured and, if you can, use it rather than vegetable oil to get a real Spanish flavour into the food. In Spain the meals start late and go on long. So, if your Paella takes longer to prepare than you anticipated, well, it will be all the more authentic!

Gazpacho

Gazpacho is not quite a salad, and not quite a soup. It's somewhere delicious in between. On a hot day it's refreshing and on a dull day it will bring a little sunshine. Tinned tomatoes work very well in Gazpacho as, with a pinch of sugar added, they often taste better than English hothouse ones.

1 large tin of tomatoes or
  1 pound (400 g) fresh
  tomatoes (cheaper squashy
  ones will be fine)
1 clove garlic
1 green pepper
1 onion

$\frac{1}{2}$ cucumber
1 tablespoon wine vinegar
1 tablespoon oil (olive oil is
  best)
Salt and pepper
A pinch of castor sugar

43

Some people make this soup by puréeing the vegetables in a blender but I think it's much better when everything is chopped into little pieces by hand. Open the tin of tomatoes and strain off the juice into a large bowl. Chop the tomatoes into small pieces. Chop finely or crush the garlic clove. Remove the core and the seeds from the green pepper and chop it into tiny squares. Peel the cucumber and chop that too. Add all these ingredients to the tomato juice plus the sugar, salt and pepper. Mix in the wine (*not* malt) vinegar and oil. You now add half a tin of cold water or 6 ice cubes, stirring until they melt. The soup should be served very cold. Little pieces of fried bread (*croûtons*) set it off nicely. If you use fresh tomatoes, follow the peeling instructions from the Paella recipe and add more water or ½ pint (3 dl) of tomato juice at the end.

Paella

Paella is probably the most famous Spanish dish and one for which there are many recipes. Although you can vary the ingredients, leaving out the ones you can't get hold of or don't like, it should never taste like a mixture of left-overs and rice! A Paella pan is like a frying-pan with two little handles but an ordinary heavy frying-pan or heatproof shallow dish will do. Here is a basic recipe and as long as you get the amount of liquid right the other ingredients can be altered to suit your taste.

2 tablespoons oil (try to use olive oil — it makes all the difference)
1 clove garlic
1 medium-size onion, chopped
1 chicken portion
2 tomatoes, fresh or from a tin
1 small packet of frozen peas
A few prawns, frozen or fresh

1 pint (6 dl) fresh mussels, *not* the ones in jars
1 red (sweet) pepper, fresh or from a tin
2 teacupfuls rice
4 teacupfuls chicken stock (use the same measure as for the rice)
A pinch of paprika
Salt and pepper

Peel the clove of garlic. Chop the red pepper, first removing the seeds from inside, into thin strips. If you are using fresh tomatoes peel by putting in a bowl and pouring boiling water over them, let them stand for a few minutes then pour off the water. You will find the skins slip off easily. Chop the peeled or tinned tomatoes. Divide the chicken into small pieces. If you are using mussels, scrub them very well under cold running water and throw out any that are open or cracked. Make up a chicken stock cube if you have no fresh stock. Heat the oil in the frying-pan and cook the clove of garlic for a minute or two to flavour the oil. Remove the garlic using a slotted spoon. Add the chopped onion, red pepper, tomatoes and chicken and stir while they fry. Sprinkle them with the paprika and fry some more, until the vegetables are soft and the chicken begins to look white and cooked. Add the rice (use long grain or medium grain but not pudding rice) and stir until it looks transparent. Take the pan off the heat and pour on the stock. Return the pan to the heat, stir well and add a

pinch of salt and pepper. When the liquid starts to boil, add the peas and prawns (you can leave fresh ones in their shells, they look so pretty) and simmer gently for about 20 minutes when most of the liquid will have been absorbed. If you have mussels, place them on top and cover the pan. The steam will open them, and if any do not open, into the dustbin with them. After a few minutes the Paella will be ready. Test a grain of rice to make sure it is tender. Serve it from the pan.

Salt Cod

Salt Cod (Bacalhau) can now be found in many delicatessens including Spanish, Italian, Greek and West Indian ones. It will either be hanging up in a piece or cut and cellophane-wrapped. There are countless Portuguese recipes for Bacalhau. This is one of the most popular and you'll see why if you try it, but you must plan the dish a day in advance as the fish has to be soaked.

BACALHAU GOMES DE SA

½ pound (200 g) dried salt cod

4 medium-size potatoes

3 tablespoons oil (preferably olive oil)

2 medium-size onions, peeled and chopped

1 clove garlic, peeled and finely chopped

2 hard-boiled eggs, sliced

6 black olives (only if you like them)

Pepper

Soak the cod in cold water for 24 hours, changing the water once or twice. Place it in a saucepan with enough water to cover it, bring to the boil and simmer for half an hour. Meanwhile peel the potatoes and halve them, trying to get the pieces all more or less the same size for even cooking. Add them to the saucepan and simmer until done, about 15–20 minutes. While this is happening hard boil the 2 eggs. Lift out the fish with a slotted strainer on to a plate. When it has cooled remove the skin and bone and flake the fish. Heat the oil in a frying-pan or casserole and fry the chopped onions and garlic until soft. Add the fish, the olives if you are including them, and sprinkle on some pepper. Strain the potatoes. Chop them roughly and add them too. Cook it all gently until heated through then decorate with the slices of hard-boiled egg.

Tortilla

Tortilla is Spanish for omelette and a Spanish omelette is quite different from a French one. It is more solid, more like an egg cake. The traditional Spanish omelette contains only potatoes and onions mixed with the eggs, but feel free to add peas, beans, chopped tomato, strips of red pepper and chopped ham to make a real meal of it.

2 large potatoes
2 medium-size onions
4 eggs

Oil for frying (preferably olive oil)
Salt and pepper

Peel the potatoes and chop them into small cubes. Peel the onions and chop them also into small pieces. Heat a tablespoon of oil in a frying-pan and add the potatoes and onions. Sprinkle with salt and fry gently stirring from time to time. Cover the frying-pan with a large saucepan lid and cook the vegetables until they are soft, removing the lid and stirring from time to time. Add a little more oil if they seem to be sticking. It will take about 20 minutes. Beat the eggs with a pinch of salt and pepper in a large bowl. Remove the potatoes and onions from the pan with

a slotted spoon and add to the eggs. If you are using any other kinds of filling add them now, and mix together. Pour off most of the oil from the pan, leaving just a thin film at the bottom. At this point turn on the grill section of your cooker. If the pan is a bit crusty with potato and onion you will have to clean it before you fry the Tortilla or it will stick and spoil the look of the dish. If you have had to clean the pan, heat up a little of the oil you have poured off in the bottom. Now pour in the egg mixture and carefully shake the pan and if necessary flatten the mixture with a fork. Cook very gently until you see the sides coming away from the edges. Now take the frying-pan and place under the grill for a few minutes until the top is cooked and golden. The Tortilla can now be cut into triangular slices and eaten hot or cold. Cold, and carefully wrapped, it's very good for a picnic.

Torrijas

This is a pudding Spanish children love. For them it would probably be cooked in olive oil but a mixture of butter and vegetable oil is probably more to your taste. See if you can persuade your mother or someone who has such things, to give you a drop of sweet sherry. You can make Torrijas without it but it's much more Spanish with it!

A few slices of bread (stale
bread will do)
2 egg yolks
1 tablespoon sweet sherry
1 ounce (25 g) butter or
margarine

1 tablespoon oil
1 tablespoon icing sugar
1 teaspoon cinnamon

Separate 2 eggs and put the yolks in a bowl with the sherry. Beat
together with an egg whisk. Pour the mixture into a soup plate or
shallow dish. Soak small slices of bread in this mixture. Mix
together the icing sugar and cinnamon. Heat the butter and oil
in a frying-pan and fry the soaked bread until crisp. Remove from
the pan and sprinkle with sugar and cinnamon while still hot.

The ARAB COUNTRIES

Couscous
Shish Kebab
Kofta
Honey and Nut Pastries
Dried Fruit Salad

Arab food is a wonderful mingling and blending of cultural, geographical and religious influences. Although in a way it is an exotic cuisine, it is mostly simply prepared and well suited to feasts and family get-togethers, a favourite occupation in these countries where hospitality is an obligation as well as a pleasure. Every meeting and transaction is dignified by the offering of food or at the very least a glass of mint tea. Shopping in Arab countries is still done mostly in the colourful bazaars and *souks* where the tempting displays of foodstuffs and ingredients give you an idea about the dishes; the meat is mainly lamb, the poultry chicken and pigeons. Tomatoes, courgettes, aubergines, onions, green beans, fresh herbs, oranges and lemons are piled high in the various stalls; different spices occupy more little shops, while others are full of the dried fruits that are often cooked with meat or used in fruit salads. Rice, whole wheat, cracked wheat, and dried beans are used much more than potatoes or pasta. The semolina called couscous is the basis for the popular dish of that name from Morocco, Algeria and Tunisia. Couscous and other dishes are often eaten without a knife or fork using the right hand (never the left) and it is a custom you might want to adopt! Desserts are usually very sweet indeed; flaky pastry wrapped around nuts and drenched in honey or syrup, not good for your teeth, but nevertheless very good!

Couscous

Couscous, which is like semolina and made from wheat, is the national dish of the Arab world. You can buy couscous now in most big supermarkets or in delicatessens and it makes an intriguing change from rice, pasta, or other staple foods that you eat with meat and vegetables. You steam couscous to cook it. A large sieve or a muslin-lined colander that will fit on top of a saucepan will work well if you don't have a proper steamer.

½ pound (200 g) couscous
2 small onions
4 carrots
2 stalks of celery
2 courgettes
2 leeks (optional)
1 tin of chick peas (optional)
A handful of raisins

1 tablespoon tomato purée
2 chicken portions or 1
   pound (400 g) lean
   stewing lamb
Chilli powder (if you like
   things hot)
Salt and pepper
1 ounce (25 g) butter

Put the couscous in a bowl and pour over it ½ pint (3 dl) of warm water. Leave for 10 minutes. The couscous will swell up. In a large saucepan about half-full with water put the chicken or lamb (trimmed of as much fat as possible), the peeled onions, scraped carrots left whole, and trimmed celery stalks. If you are using leeks, cut off the root and the green part, peel off the outer layer, and clean carefully under running water as they are often

hiding quite a lot of soil. Add a generous pinch of salt and some pepper. Bring to the boil on the stove. Using a large fine-mesh sieve or colander that will fit on to the saucepan arrange the couscous above but not touching the boiling water. Cover with a saucepan lid and let the contents of the pan simmer for 30 minutes. Remove the strainer or sieve full of couscous and stir it gently with a fork to break up any lumps. If you are using chick peas, strain them from the tin and add to the saucepan. Wash the courgettes but don't peel them, cut into large chunks and add. Add the raisins. Add the tomato purée and stir in well. Replace the couscous and simmer for another 15 minutes. Remove the couscous and turn into a heated dish. Cut up the butter into little pats and put on top. Pour the meat and vegetables and the broth into another large bowl and taste to see if more salt and pepper is needed. Serve the two bowls separately and give your friends soup bowls, a knife, a fork and a spoon. In Tunisia where they like a spicy sauce, about a cupful of stock is mixed with chilli powder and served separately so each person can season their plateful to taste.

Shish Kebab

This famous Turkish dish — an idea as sensible as the sandwich — is said to have originated during the Ottoman Empire when soldiers forced to camp outside during their wars of conquest discovered how delicious meat could be threaded on a sword and cooked over an open fire. To go one better than the soldiers you can marinate the meat for a few hours or overnight and this will make up for any flavour that might be missing due to your gas or electric stove not being a Turkish camp site !

1 pound (400 g) lamb or beef
    (tell your butcher that it is
    for kebabs and he will, with
    luck, cut it into cubes for
    you)

1 onion
Lamb's liver or chicken
    livers (which are cheaper)
    are also good cooked this
    way

Marinades:

(This means a mixture you leave the meat in for a few hours or overnight to give it flavour and make it more tender.)

Method 1:

1 cup oil (olive oil if you can spare it)
The juice of 1 lemon

A pinch of cinnamon
Salt and pepper

Mix together and pour over the meat in a small bowl. Turn the meat occasionally so it all gets its fair share.

Method 2:

1 small carton of plain yogurt
1 onion finely chopped

Salt and pepper

Follow the same instructions as for Method 1.

Peel and then chop an onion into quarters. Separate the layers. Thread skewers with a piece of meat, a piece of onion and so on. You can also add quartered tomatoes, pieces of green pepper and mushrooms if you like. Turn on the grill. Lay the loaded skewers on the grill pan and brush with some of the marinade if you have used one. Grill the meat and using oven gloves turn it once to cook the underside, brushing it with the marinade again. Total

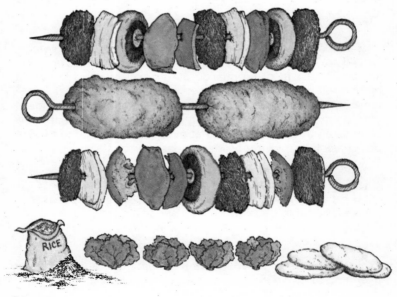

cooking time should be about 10 minutes. Serve with rice, salad or that flat Turkish bread (*pitta*) that looks like creaky bedroom slippers.

Kofta

Kofta is skewers of minced meat. Use ½ pound (200 g) minced lamb or beef. Mix it in a bowl with 1 egg yolk, 1 finely chopped onion, salt, pepper, and a pinch of ground cinnamon or ground allspice. When well mixed make it into little sausage shapes around the skewer and grill and serve as above.

Honey and Nut Pastries

Middle Eastern meals often end with, and Middle Eastern parties often revolve round, pastries made with layers of paper thin dough, steeped in honey or syrup and wrapped round crunchy nuts. There are various kinds, often named according to their shape (Bride's Fingers is one) and perhaps the best known here is Baklava. If you cannot get *fila* pastry at a Greek shop, use frozen puff pastry, thawed and rolled out as thin as you can possibly manage.

Oven time: 45 minutes
Oven setting: electric 375°F, gas No. 4

Pastry:

½ pound (200 g) *fila* pastry or 1 packet frozen puff pastry
2 ounces (50 g) butter, melted
¼ pound (100 g) nuts (walnuts, pistachio nuts or almonds coarsely chopped; a mixture of the three is nicest, but to economize chopped unsalted peanuts can be used)
1 tablespoon sugar

Syrup:

4 ounces (100 g) sugar
½ cup water
A squeeze of lemon juice
1 dessertspoon rose water or orange blossom water (optional)

Turn on the oven. You will need a pastry brush for this recipe.

Brush melted butter over the base of a small roasting tin or a cake tin. Lay on top one slice of *fila* pastry. If you are using puff pastry, divide the dough into 8 pieces and roll them out on a floured board as thinly as you can. Brush the pastry with butter, lay on another piece and repeat until you have used 4 sheets. Mix the chopped nuts and sugar together and spread that over the pastry. Lay on top the remaining sheets of pastry brushing each one with melted butter (so they will separate into layers). With the point of a sharp knife cut one way and then another to make diamond shapes on the top layer. Place on the middle shelf of the oven. Make the syrup by simmering the sugar, water and lemon juice together in a saucepan until it thickens enough to coat the back of a metal spoon. If you are using rose water or orange blossom water stir it in now. Then put the saucepan in the refrigerator or some other cold place.

When the pastry is puffed up and golden (after about 45 minutes) remove from the oven using oven gloves and pour the syrup all over it. Leave to cool. When ready to serve divide it into sections and serve from the pan.

Dried Fruit Salad

Stewed fruit, either fresh or dried, is nearly always on a Middle Eastern menu. Dried fruit needn't be thought the poor relation; it makes a delicious fruit salad in its own right. It is particularly good with the addition of nuts: almonds, pistachio nuts or pine kernels.

Use whichever dried fruits you like best – a mixture (about 1 pound [400 g] altogether) of apricots, prunes, apples, peaches, figs, raisins (health food shops usually have a good selection). Leave them to soak overnight in enough water to cover. Place them with their soaking water in a pan. If you have some nuts (blanched almonds are the best addition, I think) add them to the fruit now. Add 2 tablespoons sugar. Bring to the boil and simmer until the fruit is tender adding more water if necessary. This will take at least half an hour and maybe longer. Pour the fruit and the juice into a pretty bowl and let it cool. Serve with thick cream or yogurt and demerara sugar to sprinkle on top.

THE BALKANS and RUSSIA

Bortsch
Piroshki
Stuffed Cabbage Leaves
Yogurt

There is not enough room in this book to describe the food of every country, so in this section we can only acknowledge the Greek and Turkish influences on the Balkans — Yugoslavia, Romania and Bulgaria — to do a little justice to their food. Some similarities are still obvious — stuffed cabbage leaves appear under different names in all these countries. In general, dishes based on minced meat are popular, and one of the many kinds of bread, rather than potatoes, would be a typical accompaniment. Yogurt and raw onion are two other typical Eastern European ingredients and garnish. Yogurt or soured cream stirred into soups and stews is a delicious and healthy habit. Balkan households tend to have one hot meal a day, usually lunch, and then in the evening the same dish might be eaten cold, a labour-saving practice though one we might think a bit dull.

Russia is a huge country with extremes of climate and, not surprisingly, a wide range of foods. However, only a few dishes seem to have made themselves widely known as Russian and some of these — Chicken Kiev, Beef Stroganoff — have a somewhat unauthentic ring about them. Bortsch and Piroshki, on the other hand, you would certainly find eaten everywhere, and together they make a splendid Russian meal, which you can make even more authentic by serving a few cold tit-bits of fish or meat beforehand. In Russia these would be called *Zakusi* (hors-d'œuvres) and they are a famous part of Russian hospitality.

Bortsch

Bortsch is the famous ruby-red Russian soup made with beet-root. It can vary from a clear liquid, served with a dollop of sour cream, to a mixture of ingredients which is almost a meal in itself – though never a heavy one. Use cooked beetroots that you buy for salad, not the ones pickled in vinegar.

2 or 3 (depending on size) cooked beetroots
1 onion
2–3 carrots
2 stalks celery (optional)
1 ounce (25 g) butter

2 pints (1·2 litres) meat stock (use a beef cube if you are using cubes)
1 bay leaf
Salt and pepper

To make more of a meal of it:

½ pound (200 g) continental boiling sausage

½ a small cabbage

Chop the beetroots into small cubes. Peel and slice the onion and carrots and chop the celery. Melt the butter in a fairly large saucepan and cook the chopped onion until it is soft and beginning to turn golden. Add the beetroots, carrots and celery and stir

around until they are coated in butter. Add the stock, the bay leaf and a pinch of salt and pepper, bring to the boil and simmer gently for 35 minutes. Taste to see if it needs more salt and pepper. There are now four things you can do. Eat the soup hot as it is. Strain it and eat it hot. Strain it and cool it and use it as a cold summer soup (lovely with a spoonful of sour cream). Or to make a more substantial dish you can add sliced sausage and chopped cabbage and cook for another 10 minutes and serve hot with wholemeal (or black) bread and butter. Piroshki, see the recipe on page 61, go very well with bortsch.

Piroshki

Pir in Russian means feast and Piroshki, which are little meat pies, can make a feast of soup, of any meal where they are the first course, or of a snack anytime. They can be made with short-crust or puff pastry but I think puff pastry is lighter and nicer. The fillings can be meat or fish or vegetables and there is no reason why you shouldn't make up your own.

Oven time: 20 minutes
Oven setting: electric 425°F, gas No. 7

1 packet frozen puff pastry

One filling:

1 cup cooked rice	Salt and pepper
2 hard-boiled eggs	A couple of sprigs of parsley
2 ounces (50 g) mushrooms	or dill (optional)
½ ounce (12 g) butter or oil	

Slice the mushrooms and fry them in the butter until they are cooked through. Mix them with the rice, chopped eggs, chopped herbs (if you have them) and salt and pepper.

Another filling:

½ pound (200 g) minced beef	2 hard-boiled eggs
	1 chopped onion
1 ounce (25 g) butter or oil	Salt and pepper

Melt the butter or oil in a frying-pan and fry the chopped onion until it is soft. Add the minced beef and fry until it is brown. Off the heat, mix in the chopped hard-boiled eggs, salt and pepper.

Turn on the oven. Roll out the puff pastry according to the instructions on the packet. With a 3-inch (7-cm) biscuit cutter or rim of a teacup cut out as many circles as you can. Gather up the scraps of pastry and roll them out again and get some more circles. Put heaped teaspoons of whatever filling you have made in the centre of each circle of dough. Fold the dough over into a shape like a half moon and press the edges of the dough firmly together. With a spatula lift the little pies on to a baking sheet and bake in the centre of the oven. These can be eaten hot or cold, when they would be ideal picnic food.

Stuffed Cabbage Leaves

Dolmas and *samarle* are the Greek and Romanian for stuffed cabbage leaves (though the Greeks often use vine leaves and the Romanians frequently first pickle the cabbage leaves). Anyway they are central to Central European cooking and cheap and easy to make.

 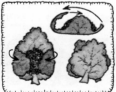 

1 cup cooked rice
½ pound (200 g) minced beef
  or lamb
1 medium-sized onion
A pinch of dried herbs or 1
  dessertspoon chopped
  fresh parsley

Salt and pepper
A squeeze of lemon juice
8 large outer leaves of a
  green cabbage
2 tablespoons vegetable oil
  (olive oil if you can spare it)

Mix all the ingredients, except the cabbage leaves and the oil, in a bowl, stirring well with a fork. Put the cabbage leaves in a baking tin and pour boiling water over them. Leave them to soak and soften for a few minutes then carefully tip the water away. Take out the cabbage leaves and lay them on the table. Put a heap of filling on each leaf and roll it up like a parcel, tucking the sides in first. Arrange the parcels in a large pan with the 'join' of the leaf underneath. Boil 1 pint (6 dl) water with the oil and a pinch of salt and pour over the cabbage parcels. Simmer very gently for 45 minutes then lift the dolmas from the pan with a slotted spoon. These are good served with a tomato sauce.

Yogurt

People who live to a ripe old age in the Balkans are said to do so because of the amount of yogurt they consume. So start making your own now (so easy and much cheaper than buying it) and who knows, you too might live to be an energetic hundred. Use ordinary plain yogurt to get yours started (it doesn't have to be 'live') and flavour it, if you want to, with honey and fruit and nuts. Plain it's very good served with the Stuffed Cabbage Leaves on page 62.

1 pint (6 dl) homogenized milk	2 heaped teaspoons plain yogurt

Heat the milk in a saucepan until it starts to rise in the pan and very nearly boil. This is what is meant by scalding milk. Remove from the stove and leave it to cool until it is tepid, that is neither hot nor cold to the touch, in fact about your blood temperature. Pour it into a china or earthenware bowl or jug in which you have put the 2 teaspoons of the bought yogurt. Mix very well. Cover it somewhere warm, like an airing cupboard or above the stove, and leave at least 6 hours or preferably overnight. By then it will have thickened and turned into a pint (6 dl) of yogurt. Two teaspoons of this can be used to make another batch and so on, until you find it becoming a bit thin. Then you must buy another carton of shop yogurt and start again.

SCANDINAVIA and The NETHERLANDS

Smorrebrod
Split Pea Soup
Frikadeller
Jansson's Temptation
Spiced Biscuits

Denmark, Sweden, Norway, Finland and Holland are a lot of countries to lump together under one heading. But a fish swimming between them would be much appreciated by each one of these countries. It might be served simply with a sauce of melted butter, or it might be pickled, salted, smoked or cured in some other way. Fish and seafood are an important part of the Scandinavian diet, and herrings in particular are treated in dozens of different ways. So popular are they, that they're often sold in the street as snacks. In Holland, milk, butter and cheese feature strongly. A Dutch breakfast might include cheese — probably a nice, round, red, shiny Edam — cold meats, eggs and a variety of breads. Substantial breakfasts are usually followed by lighter lunches, often the open sandwiches that we connect with Denmark and Sweden. Soups, light ones and the hearty meal-in-one kind, are popular. Maybe the best dessert is fresh berries with cream followed by a mouthful of dark Dutch chocolate! Christmas is celebrated with great care and elaboration in all these countries, and the spiced biscuits are something you could easily make part of your own Christmas eating and decorations.

Smorrebrod

Smorrebrod is a Danish word meaning bread and butter, but with good things on top or, to put it another way, open sandwiches. It's a sensible way of feeding yourself and your friends as there is not so much bread (to make you fat) and you can use your skill and imagination making the sandwiches look pretty.

If you are making a selection, as you might for a party, try using different breads as a base — dark rye bread is particularly tasty and authentic. Butter the slices carefully and right to the edge as, if the sandwiches have to sit around a while, this helps stop the bread becoming soggy. Get ready a selection of toppings. You might use:

Slices of cheese
Slices of ham, salami, garlic
    sausage or cold meat
Sardines
Tuna fish
Pâté
Slices of hard-boiled egg
Slices of tomato
Lettuce leaves
Fresh spinach leaves

Grated carrot
Apple slices or grated apple
Crisply fried bacon
Chopped parsley
Slices of raw mushroom
Stalks of celery
Mayonnaise for spreading on
    the bread in place of butter
    or blobbing on top of the
    sandwiches

Some of the Danish open sandwiches have names. For instance:

HANS ANDERSEN
Rye bread spread with liver pâté and topped with bacon, tomato and horseradish.

TIVOLI
Cover bread in lettuce. Arrange a lengthwise row of slices of hard-boiled egg and alongside slices of tomato. Pipe mayonnaise down the centre.

DANE'S DELIGHT
Cover bread with sliced pork. Mound some pickled red cabbage on top. Place a twist of orange on top and some pieces of crisp crackling if available.

OLIVER TWIST
Two slices pork luncheon meat folded on the bread. Spoon on some horseradish sauce. Tuck in a sprig of parsley.

MASTER MARINER
Butter bread. Arrange three pieces of pickled herring diagonally across the bread. Decorate with onion rings and parsley.

Why not christen your own creations?

Split Plea Soup

The harsh winters in Holland have some compensations — ponds frozen over for skating and hearty meal-in-one soups to warm up with. A spoon should almost stand up in this mixture of meat, dried peas and vegetables.

½ pound (200 g) split green peas (left to soak overnight in a bowl of water)
1 small piece of uncooked ham or bacon (sometimes you can get cheap cuts in the supermarket)

1 onion
1 leek
A few stalks of celery (optional)
A pinch of pepper
A piece of boiling ring or other spicy sausage

If you haven't soaked the peas overnight, here is what to do. Put them in a saucepan of water, bring to the boil, boil for 10 minutes then remove the pan from the stove and let the peas cool in the water. Drain them. They will take a bit longer to cook than the soaked ones, but not for ever. In a saucepan put the peas, the ham and the onion which you have peeled and sliced. Cover with 2 pints (1·2 litres) of water and bring to the boil, then simmer until the peas are soft (this may take an hour). Chop the celery and leek and add to the soup. Add the boiling ring or sausage and cook for another half an hour. Carefully remove the sausage, slice it, and return it to the soup. Taste the soup to see if it needs more salt (the ham may have salted it enough) and add some pepper. Serve it in bowls with lots of brown bread and butter to eat with it.

Frikadeller

Frikadeller are meatballs made with minced veal. Some super-markets sell minced veal now but a helpful butcher would mince you some stewing veal if you can't find it ready done. These little morsels, very popular in Denmark, are lighter and more delicate than beef meatballs and if you like yogurt or soured cream, a little spooned in at the end makes a delicious sauce.

$\frac{1}{2}$ pound (200 g) minced
  veal including some fat
2 thick slices of stale white
  bread
1 small onion, chopped
A sprinkling of herbs (thyme
  is good but parsley will do)

$\frac{1}{4}$ pint (1·5 dl) of milk
About 1 heaped tablespoon
  flour
Carton of soured cream or
  plain yogurt (optional)
Salt and pepper
1 tablespoon cooking oil.

Remove the crusts from the bread and in a shallow dish soak the bread in the milk. When it is well soaked in, with very *clean* hands, squeeze out bread and crumble into a bowl. Add the veal,

the chopped onion, the herbs and a generous pinch of salt and pepper. With your hands (still clean I hope) mix all the ingredients well, adding a little of the soaking milk if necessary. Roll the mixture into small balls, about the size of a giant marble and roll them on a plate on which you have sprinkled flour. They should be just lightly dusted with flour. Heat the oil in a large frying-pan and fry the meatballs until brown. If you like the idea of the yogurt or soured cream, add it when the Frikadeller are cooked through and just gently shake the pan whilst it heats through. Don't boil the yogurt as it will separate. Serve straight from the pan. Nice with rice.

Jansson's Temptation

You may sometimes have wondered what you can do with those little flat tins of anchovies. This is one of the *best* things you can do with one and the combination of potatoes, onions, anchovies and cream would tempt anyone — even those who think anchovies are a bit fishy!

Oven time: 45 minutes
Oven setting: electric 400°F, gas No. 6

1 small tin of anchovies	1 small carton of single cream
1 pound (400 g) potatoes	1 ounce (25 g) butter
2 medium or 1 large onion	Pepper

Turn on the oven. Peel the potatoes and grate them, either on the large holes of a hand grater or use a Moulinex grater with a medium blade. Tip the grated potatoes into a bowl of cold water

to stop them turning a nasty greyish-brown. Peel the onions. Halve them and slice them, flat side down, as finely as you can manage. Open the tin of anchovies. If you think they might be too salty for your taste, soak the little fillets in a saucerful of milk, but if you like quite sharp-tasting dishes, don't bother with that step. Using half the butter, grease a small casserole dish. Wring out the grated potatoes in a *clean* tea-towel or pour off the water and pat them dry with paper towels. Arrange a thin layer of potatoes in the dish, scatter on some of the onion and then lay on a few pieces of anchovy. Repeat until you have used up all the ingredients finishing with a layer of potatoes. Sprinkle some pepper over the top (you won't need salt), dot with the rest of the butter, then pour the cream on top. Place on the middle shelf of the oven and leave for 45 minutes or until the potatoes are cooked. It makes a lovely supper dish.

Spiced Biscuits

Spiced biscuits to eat with tea and coffee are popular all over the Netherlands and Scandinavia and always appear on 5 December, the feast of St Nicholas. They are often cut into fancy shapes or pressed in moulds. You can use biscuit cutters or cut round a cardboard shape that you have designed – or do a few abstract designs ! They will all taste good.

Oven time : 10 minutes (each batch of biscuits)
Oven setting : electric 375°F, gas No. 5

4 ounces (100 g) butter or margarine
2 ounces (50 g) castor sugar
2 ounces (50 g) soft brown sugar

8 ounces (200 g) plain flour
1 teaspoon mixed ground spice
1 small egg

Turn on the oven. Cream the butter (or margarine) and sugars together, either with a wooden spoon or using an electric mixer. Stir in the egg which you have first beaten in a small bowl. Sift in the flour and the spice and mix to a firm dough. You may have to use your *clean* hands as it will be quite stiff. Grease and flour a baking sheet. Roll out the dough thinly and make your shapes. Lift them carefully on to the baking sheet and when you have used all the available space place it near the top of the oven and bake for 10 minutes. Using oven gloves, remove the baking tin, lift off the biscuits with a spatula and leave to cool on a wire rack. They will become crisp as they get cold. If you have dough left over, start on the next batch, with maybe some different shapes.

INDIA and PAKISTAN

Tandoori Chicken Legs
Pulao
Egg Curry
Potato Balls

To many people Indian food means curry, and curry often means yesterday's meat heated up in a hot tasting sauce that gets its flavour from a tinned powder. This is perhaps the most wicked misunderstanding about food of all. India and Pakistan have a marvellous cuisine that has been influenced over the centuries by the Babylonians, Persians, Greeks, Huns, Mongols and more, and last, but not least, the British. However, now that the spices for making Indian food are becoming readily available here, it is time to undo any damage due to us ! Although one of the recipes in this section uses tinned curry powder, the others use separate spices which demonstrate some of the subtle flavours of Indian food, and show that it is not necessarily chilli hot. There are endless regional variations in the food of India and Pakistan, but roughly speaking there is more meat eaten in the north and greater reliance on wheat and breads, and a tendency towards vegetarianism in the south and a higher consumption of rice. Tandoori cooking, using a special vertical clay oven, is now found all over India and Pakistan and is one of the most delicious ways of preparing meat. Indian cooking is basically home cooking, as to be done really well it requires a lot of preparation. In your home, one main dish can be made more Indian in style by preparing various side dishes, e.g. sliced onion, nuts, yogurt mixed with mint, sliced banana, mango chutney. For a drink try Lassi, made from yogurt (recipe in the section on the Balkans and Russia) thinned down with milk and ice water. Very refreshing !

Tandoori Chicken Legs

A tandoor is a clay oven used in India for roasting. It is shaped rather like a well and the food to be cooked is threaded on long skewers which are then dropped in.

Sometimes bread called *Naan* is cooked on the side of the tandoor. The nearest equivalent is an open fire or barbecue but good results can be obtained with a rotisserie in the oven or plain roasting in the oven will do. Using just the chicken legs, as in this recipe, we can cook them under the grill making them easier to baste. The longer you can leave the chicken mixture in the yogurt marinade the more tender and delicious it will be.

4 chicken legs (wings, or other pieces, of course, will do)
$\frac{1}{2}$ teaspoon salt

$\frac{1}{2}$ teaspoon pepper
$\frac{1}{2}$ teaspoon cayenne pepper
2 dessertspoons lemon juice

Marinade:

1 small carton of plain yogurt
$\frac{1}{2}$ teaspoon powdered ginger (or if you can get it about 1 inch [25 mm] fresh ginger root peeled and chopped)

2 cloves garlic
A pinch of ground coriander
A pinch of ground cumin
1 tablespoon lemon juice
A pinch of salt

Take the skin off the chicken and with the point of a sharp knife make little slashes in the flesh. Mix together the lemon juice, salt, pepper and cayenne and rub this mixture well into the chicken pushing it into the cuts. Put the chicken in a shallow dish while you mix the marinade. Empty the yogurt into a bowl. If you have fresh ginger, chop it very finely. Peel and chop the garlic cloves finely or push them through a garlic press. Add to the yogurt with the lemon juice, salt, coriander and cumin. Mix well. Pour this over the chicken and put in the fridge or other cool place for a few hours, or, better still, overnight. When you are ready to cook the chicken, turn on the grill and arrange the pieces on the pan. Grill under medium heat, basting the pieces from time to time with the marinade. Use oven gloves when you pull out the grill pan to do this. After 15 to 20 minutes when the meat should be cooked through turn up the grill to high to crisp the outside of the chicken pieces. These are delicious hot or cold, eaten on their own or with rice and salad.

Pulao

Pulaos and Birianis (however you spell them) are Moghlai dishes using spices and butter to enrich and flavour rice. They can be cooked with meat, fish or vegetables but a plain Pulao with raisins and almonds is delicious and if you want to add meat, for instance left-over lamb, beef or chicken, or vegetables like peas or grated raw carrot, you can do so using the basic recipe

below. Add them along with the spices. It is important to use a good variety of rice. Basmati rice is the best but in any case make sure you have a long-grain rice and wash it well to remove extra starch. The idea is to end up with each grain separate, not a spicy rice pudding!

1 large teacupful of long-
  grain rice
1 onion finely chopped
½ inch (12 mm) cinnamon
  stick broken into pieces
8 whole cardamoms
4 cloves
1 bay leaf broken into bits

2 ounces (50 g) butter
Salt and pepper
¼ teaspoon turmeric
  (optional)
1 tablespoon raisins
1 tablespoon blanched
  almonds

Wash the rice in a sieve to rinse off any starchiness clinging to it. Peel and chop the onion finely. Melt the butter in a saucepan and fry the onion until it is soft, then add the spices and stir them around (turmeric if you use it will turn the rice a lovely yellow colour), then the rice. Cook gently, stirring all the time, until the rice is well coated with butter and begins to look transparent. Using the same cup that you used to measure the rice add 2 cupfuls of water and a pinch of salt and pepper. Bring to the boil. Cover the pan and simmer on a low heat, checking every now and then to see if you need to add a little more water. The idea is that when the rice is cooked all the water should be absorbed and the rice dry and fluffy. When the rice is ready (it takes about 15 minutes) turn it into a dish and keep warm in the oven. In the rinsed out pan quickly fry the almonds and raisins in a pat of butter. Add them to the Pulao and serve.

Egg Curry

Although curries are far and away better when you make them with freshly ground spices mixed yourself, there are times when it's certainly easier to use ready-made curry powder. Make sure the tin you use is reasonably newly bought, as curry powder once opened goes stale. The Hindus believe that the universe emerged from the cosmic egg, or egg of Brahman. So!

4 hard-boiled eggs
1 ounce (25 g) butter
1 onion
1 dessertspoon curry powder
1 dessertspoon flour
½ pint (3 dl) stock made from
    a chicken stock cube

2 tomatoes sliced
1 heaped teaspoon mango
    chutney
A squeeze of lemon juice

Peel and chop the onion and fry it in a saucepan in the melted
butter. Add the curry powder and stir it around to cook it for a
few minutes (important). Add the flour and stir until blended.
Pour on the stock bit by bit, stirring carefully to avoid any lumps
forming. When it has all been added bring the sauce to the boil
and simmer for 15 to 20 minutes. Add the chutney and stir. Taste
to see if you need salt, add the sliced tomatoes and a squeeze of
lemon, leave to simmer while you peel and halve the eggs. Lay
them in the sauce and heat through very gently. Serve with plain
boiled rice and more mango chutney.

Potato Balls

Alu means potato and *kofta* means vegetable ball so this dish is
called *Alu Kofta.* Vegetable balls are a good way of using any
left-over cooked vegetables you have and they make a meal on
their own or a good snack. You can also serve the Koftas with the
curry sauce described above in the Egg Curry recipe.

1 pound (400 g) potatoes
1 small onion or 4 spring
  onions
1 cup cooked peas (or other
  vegetable like cauliflower,
  spinach, cabbage)
1 tablespoon chopped
  coriander leaves (or parsley
  or celery leaves if you
  cannot get coriander)

1 teaspoon garam masala (a
  spice mixture in a tin easily
  found in shops)
A squeeze of lemon juice
A pinch of salt and pepper
Vegetable oil for frying
Some plain flour

Peel the potatoes and boil them in salted water until they are well cooked. Strain them and mash them. Mix in the other ingredients and roll the mixture into about 25 small balls. Dust the balls all over with plain flour. Heat the oil in a large frying-pan and fry the Koftas until they are golden brown.

CHINA and JAPAN

Spare Ribs

Chow Mein

Stir-fried Chicken with
   Green Beans

Cos Lettuce or Chinese
   Cabbage in Cream Sauce

Tempura

China has perhaps the most dishes of any country. If you were to collect all the recipes — an impossible task since many would not be written down — there would be tens of thousands. This is partly to do with the fact that the Chinese relish all food (there is almost nothing edible that isn't eaten) and they enjoy each part for its own qualities ; the crispiness of roasted skin, the sponginess of cooked dried mushroom, the nibbliness of little bones. Fish heads and duck's feet are, for instance, two quite common ingredients. Add to that the fact that they have so many different techniques of cooking — stir-frying, steaming, crystal boiling, clear simmering, wind-drying, smoking, red cooking, to name a few — and that some dishes are cooked using two or more of these processes and you begin to realize the scope of Chinese food. The time spent in making the food is often largely in its preparation, then it is cooked very quickly, which is economical on fuel. Stir-frying, where the ingredients are chopped small and then fried quickly in oil, usually in a bowl-shaped frying-pan called a *Wok*, is the first Chinese technique to master. Meals in China, even simple family ones, usually have at least five or six different dishes with everyone helping themselves to a bit of each. But until you have got used to all the last-minute activity, do just one main dish with some boiled rice or noodles. You could try growing your own bean sprouts (any dampened dried bean or pea will sprout) to use for a vegetable. The most striking thing about Japanese food is the artistry with which it is prepared and presented. It is always served simply and elegantly and on beautiful ceramic or wooden dishes. Fish, vegetables and rice are the main ingredients. It is an austere, healthy way of eating.

Spare Ribs

Barbecued spare ribs are probably one of the most frequently ordered dishes in Chinese restaurants. It is hard to resist the appeal of gnawing on such tasty bones ! The basis of the sauce is sweet (honey) and sour (vinegar) with other flavours such as garlic, ginger and soya sauce added. When you understand this principle you can make your own barbecue sauce with whatever you have on hand. You can roast a rack of ribs in one piece or ask your butcher to chop them for you. The Chinese often chop them into 1-inch (25-mm) lengths to serve as a first course.

Oven time: 1 hour
Oven setting: electric 350°F, gas No. 4

1 rack of American-style pork
  spare ribs
½ tin of clear beef consommé
2 tablespoons soya sauce
1 dessertspoon honey
1 heaped teaspoon brown
  sugar

1 tablespoon wine vinegar
1 clove garlic, peeled and
  finely chopped
A pinch of salt and pepper

Turn on the oven. Place the spare ribs flat in a baking tray not too much bigger than the ribs. Mix the consommé and other ingredients in a saucepan, heat up and simmer for a few minutes. Pour the sauce over the ribs in the tin and place on the middle shelf of the oven. Roast the ribs, removing the tin from time to time (wearing oven gloves) to spoon the sauce over the meat. Fifteen minutes before their time is up increase the oven heat to 450°F or gas No. 7 to brown and crisp them. The sauce should almost have disappeared and the ribs should be glossy and a lovely deep brown colour. Serve on their own or with rice.

Chow Mein

Chow Mein means fried noodles and the phrase — and the dish — sometimes covers a multitude of sins. It is worth selecting the ingredients carefully and seasoning them correctly so you don't have a mish-mash but a genuine Chinese flavour. Chinese noodles, available in large supermarkets and Oriental groceries, are best for this dish but if you can't get them use egg noodles (e.g. tagliatelle) rather than spaghetti.

½ pound (200 g) Chinese noodles
½ pound (200 g) lean pork or chicken
3 Chinese dried mushrooms (or ordinary mushrooms if necessary)
2 tablespoons vegetable oil
3 spring onions
3 ounces (75 g) shredded cabbage or ¼ pound (100 g) bean sprouts
1 tablespoon soya sauce
Salt and pepper
½ teaspoon sugar

Cook the noodles in boiling salted water until just tender, drain, rinse under the cold tap and set aside. Slice the meat into small shreds. Put the dried mushrooms in a bowl and pour on boiling water. Let stand for 15 to 30 minutes then drain and chop into strips. *Or* slice fresh mushrooms. Heat 1 tablespoon of oil in a frying-pan, add the spring onions chopped into 1-inch (25-mm) pieces, and the cabbage. Stir for 2 minutes then lift out and set aside. Add a little more oil, if necessary, and fry the mushrooms and meat for 3 minutes. Add the soya sauce and sugar and mix well. Remove the meat and mushrooms with a slotted spoon and

set aside. Add a little more oil and fry the noodles mixing in the gravy that is in the pan. Return the meat and vegetables and heat through carefully. Taste and add salt and pepper if necessary. Serve in a heated dish.

Stir-fried Chicken with Green Beans

One of the great advantages of Chinese cooking is the speed at which many things are cooked. Quick-fried or stir-fried dishes can be cooked in minutes (though the preparation takes longer) and this is not only convenient but healthy too as precious vitamins are not cooked out nor thrown away. You can vary the vegetables in this dish to please yourself. Mange-tout peas are good, so is broccoli.

2 chicken portions or half a
  chicken
$\frac{1}{2}$ pound (200 g) French
  beans, fresh or frozen
  (runner beans would do at
  a pinch)
1 tablespoon cornflour
1 tablespoon water
3 tablespoons chicken stock

4 dried Chinese mushrooms
  or $\frac{1}{4}$ pound (100 g) fresh
  mushrooms
1 tablespoon soya sauce
1 teaspoon vinegar
1 teaspoon sugar
Salt and pepper
Vegetable oil for frying

Cut the chicken off the bones and cut further into small bite-size

84

pieces. Clean fresh beans and chop into 2-inch (50-mm) lengths or chop frozen beans. Pour boiling water over the dried mushrooms. Leave for 15 to 30 minutes then slice. *Or* slice fresh mushrooms. Mix the cornflour in a bowl with 1 tablespoon water until you have a smooth cream. Stir in the soya sauce then add the chicken and mix well to coat all the pieces. Heat one tablespoon oil in a frying-pan and add the chicken and stir-fry over a high heat for 3 or 4 minutes. With a slotted spoon remove the chicken and put on a plate. Add a little more oil and stir-fry the beans and mushrooms for 4 to 5 minutes (longer if the beans are fresh) until they are cooked but still crisp. Return the chicken to the pan. Add the chicken stock, sugar, vinegar, salt and pepper and stir-fry for another minute or two until everything is heated through and well blended. Serve hot with noodles or rice.

Cos Lettuce or Chinese Cabbage in Creamy Sauce

The Chinese are well known for cooking their vegetables quickly, in oil and very little liquid — and an excellent idea it is too, much nicer and better for you. This makes a delicious vegetable worth eating on its own.

1 Cos lettuce or ½ a head of Chinese cabbage (creeping into supermarkets these days, often called Chinese leaves)
½ cup milk
½ cup chicken stock
1 tablespoon cornflour
2 tablespoons vegetable oil
½ teaspoon sugar
A pinch of salt
1 dessertspoon dripping (chicken fat or duck fat is best)

Clean and trim the lettuce or Chinese cabbage and cut into 4-inch (100-mm) lengths. Mix the milk, chicken stock and salt in a bowl. Ladle about 3 tablespoons of that mixture into a small bowl and mix in the cornflour until you have a smooth thin cream. Heat the oil in a frying-pan, add the leaves and cook, stirring, for a minute. Add the sugar and a pinch of salt and stir for another minute. Pour in the milk and stock mixture. Bring to the boil. Stir the cornflour mixture and add it to the pan. When the sauce has thickened, switch off the heat and add the dripping. Stir once more. Adjust seasoning. Serve very hot.

Tempura

Tempura is a meal deep-fried in batter – rather like an extremely elegant version of fish and chips. Although huge prawns are customarily one of the ingredients these are so expensive that we will use fillets of plaice instead. The vegetables can be varied according to what you have, but do try deep-frying parsley – it's wonderful! Some people say that Tempura is a dish introduced into Japanese cuisine to please Westerners, others that it was brought to Japan by the Portuguese traders and missionaries in the sixteenth century. I prefer the second theory.

2 fillets of plaice cut in half lengthways and then across
4 large mushrooms' caps
1 onion
1 green pepper
1 small aubergine
4 parsley sprigs washed and dried
Vegetable oil for deep-frying
Soya sauce (to use as a dip)

Batter:

½ pint (3 dl) iced water
5 ounces plain flour
1 large egg

Peel and quarter the onion and separate the layers. Take the

seeds and pith out of the green pepper, trim round the stalk, and cut the pepper into 1-inch (25-mm) squares. Slice the aubergine in $\frac{1}{4}$-inch (6-mm) slices. Wash and dry the parsley. Arrange the fish and vegetables on a large plate. Beat together the iced water and egg and pour on to the flour which you have sifted into a bowl. Mix only very briefly until just blended. In a large saucepan pour in oil until it is about 3 inches (75 mm) deep. Heat to 375°F on a frying thermometer or until a teaspoon of batter dropped in sinks and then rises to the surface. Starting with the fish dip each ingredient into the batter and then lower into the oil with a long-handled spoon (to prevent splashes). Fry until crisp but only a pale golden colour. Cook only a few items at a time and drain on paper towels. Eat them in stages or keep the first batches warm in the oven until you finish frying. Give everyone a little bowl of soya sauce to dip the Tempura into.

Note: Remember that hot oil can burn you badly, so make sure an adult is around in case something goes wrong. Deep-frying can also be rather a smelly business! If you shut the kitchen door and open the window you will be even more popular when you serve up your Tempura.

NORTH AMERICA and CANADA

Southern Fried Chicken
Boston Baked Beans
Potato Salad
Apple Brown Betty
Blueberry Muffins

The United States and Canada are among the most fortunate countries in the abundance of produce that can be, and is, cultivated and farmed. They are big countries and eating is done on a big scale. In between meals there are snacks and in between snacks there are drinks like milk shakes and sodas. But as well as the fast food such as hamburgers, hot dogs, pizzas and triple-decker sandwiches that we think of as typically American, there is a real American cuisine that reflects the history of the many different nationalities of settlers and immigrants. There is, too, the influence of the indigenous American Indian and the African slaves, particularly on the cooking of the American South. To a certain extent, regional variations can still be found. There is the slightly puritanical fare of New England featuring many boiled dishes, sustaining meals like Boston Baked Beans, and, of course, the famous Thanksgiving Turkey. In Pennsylvania there remains a tradition of hearty Dutch and German cooking, whilst New Orleans reflects the Spanish and French influence. In the West besides, of course, a lot of beef eating, you will come across a Mexican fieriness in the food. The Pacific Coast with its ideal climate encourages a rather more exotic style of cooking. In the land of the supermarket, with frozen, packet, instant-mix food, it is still possible to get back to the delicious roots of this hard-to-define country. In Canada the main culinary difference is due to the French influence dating from the original settlers in Quebec. The more remote northern parts of Canada still offer an explorer's or trapper's life with game and fish to be hunted and simply cooked – a far cry from a TV dinner.

Southern Fried Chicken

Southern Fried Chicken seems as American as Blueberry Pie, or maybe Blueberry Pie is as American as Southern Fried Chicken. Anyway like almost any popular dish there is a good version and a terrible mass-produced version. Do it this way and you may never darken the door of a Take-Away shop again !

2 chicken portions (leg and breast *or* 2 packets of chicken wings or chicken drumsticks
4 tablespoons flour
1 teaspoon salt
1 teaspoon pepper
A pinch of cayenne pepper
6 tablespoons cooking oil *or* 4 ounces lard
½ pint (3 dl) milk

Put 3 tablespoons flour, and the salt, pepper and cayenne pepper into a strong paper bag. Add the chicken pieces. Close the top of the bag tightly and give it a good shake. Heat the oil or lard in a frying-pan and when it is hot, but before it is smoking, add the floured chicken pieces, and brown them first on one side and then on the other. Lower the heat a little and fry them gently for about 20 minutes or until when pierced with the tip of a knife the juices run clear, not pink. Take the chicken pieces out, drain them on kitchen paper, and keep them warm in a low oven while you make the milk gravy which is what makes Fried Chicken Southern. Pour off most of the fat from the frying-pan leaving

about 1 tablespoon and the crusty little bits (don't let them escape). Add 1 tablespoon flour and stir it around with a wooden spoon until it is well blended with the fat. Gradually add the milk, stirring all the time until you have a smooth and not too thick gravy. You may not need all the milk or you may need a little more. Add a pinch of salt and pepper to the gravy. You can then replace the chicken pieces in the pan and bring it to the table just like that.

Boston Baked Beans

Long before the first white man arrived in America the bean (that is what we think of as the dried bean) was being cultivated by the North American Indians. Boston Baked Beans, probably the most famous of the dried white bean recipes, was originally made with maple syrup and then with molasses. I find that treacle gives a good rich colour and is not oversweet. Try these. You might have thought baked beans only came out of tins.

Oven time : 1 hour 15 minutes
Oven setting : electric 350°F, gas No. 4

1 pound (400 g) white (haricot) dried beans, soaked (see recipe)
½ pound (200 g) salt pork or a knuckle boiling bacon
2 teaspoons salt
1 teaspoon pepper
1 tablespoon treacle
1 dessertspoon brown sugar
½ teaspoon dry mustard
1 tablespoon tomato purée or tomato ketchup

You can soak the beans overnight in cold water or if this requires too much forethought, put them in a pan and cover them well with water. Bring them to the boil, simmer for 20 minutes, then let them stand for an hour. Drain them, put them back in the pan and cover with fresh water. On the stove bring the beans to the boil, then simmer for 1–1½ hours. Cut the salt pork into small chunks leaving the rind on as this gives richness to the dish. Drain the cooked beans, keeping the water. Put the beans into an earthenware pot or other ovenproof casserole and either mix in the salt pork cubes or bury the bacon knuckle in the middle. Mix about 1 pint (6 dl) of the beans' water with all the seasonings and pour over the beans. If the liquid doesn't come to the top of the

91

beans, add a little more. Cover and place in the oven. After one hour remove the cover, using oven gloves, and let the beans bake another 15 minutes so a crust forms on the top.

Potato Salad

There are many ways of approaching making a potato salad. One of the least pleasant would be to mix cold cooked potatoes with salad cream, but that is what most bought potato salads taste like. Prince Edward Island in Canada is famous for its potatoes and if this recipe for a warm potato salad originated there, then it should be famous for that too.

1 pound (400 g) small
potatoes (the kidney-
shaped ones available in
the early summer are best)
3 rashers of bacon
3 spring onions

1 stick of celery (optional)
2 tablespoons wine vinegar
1 teaspoon salt
1 teaspoon pepper
1 tablespoon vegetable oil

The point of making warm potato salad is that the just drained hot potatoes soak up the dressing and so become laden with flavour. Scrub the potatoes (don't peel them though) and put them in a pan full of water with a teaspoon of salt and cook until they are just tender but not falling apart. If they are small this will be about 15 minutes. While they are cooking, fry the bacon until crisp, remove it, drain on kitchen paper and crumble it. Keep the bacon fat hot in the pan. Clean and finely slice the spring onions (or you can use a small ordinary onion, or even better a shallot or two). Chop into tiny squares the stick of celery if you are using it. Slice the potatoes and mix them in a bowl with the crumbled bacon, the onion and the celery. Remove the bacon fat from the heat and add the oil, vinegar, salt and pepper. Mix and pour over the potatoes, turning them carefully in the dressing. Serve right away. It's very good with cold meat.

If you prefer a creamier potato salad, use 3 tablespoons oil mixed with the vinegar and seasonings (leaving out the bacon fat) and when this dressing has soaked into the potatoes and they have become cool, mix in enough of a good brand of mayonnaise to coat the potatoes thinly.

Apple Brown Betty

Johnny Appleseed is a legendary character who travelled around the American Mid-West during the Frontier days distributing his apple-seeds, from which pips a big industry has grown. A famous American apple-based recipe is Apple Brown Betty. Johnny's Mother perhaps?

4 ounces (100 g) fresh breadcrumbs (please don't use those orange ones from a packet)

1 pound (400 g) dessert apples *or* 2 large cooking apples (Bramleys)

3 ounces (75 g) butter or margarine

4 ounces (100 g) sugar, white or brown (6 ounces [150 g] for cooking apples)

A pinch of cinnamon

Oven time: 45 minutes
Oven setting: electric 350°F, gas No. 4

Toast the breadcrumbs in a low oven, or if you watch them very carefully, spread out in the grill pan under a medium heat from the grill. Peel the apples. Core them and cut them into thin slices. Mix the sugar and cinnamon. Cut the butter into small pieces. Using one piece of the butter, grease a small ovenproof baking dish. Arrange a thin layer of crumbs, then one of apples, then sugar, then butter, crumbs, apples, sugar, butter, apples and finish with crumbs and sugar. Dot the top with any remaining butter. Bake in the oven for 45 minutes or until the apples are tender and the top is brown and crisp. Lovely with cream.

Blueberry Muffins

Although blueberries are beginning to be on sale here, they are expensive. Blackberries could be used just as well, and they have the great advantage of being free. Of course bilberries, if you can find them, would be perfect. Blueberry muffins are lovely for breakfast and just as nice for tea. They should be eaten hot from the oven but it is unlikely there would be any given even half a chance to get cold !

Oven time : 20–25 minutes
Oven setting : electric 425°F, gas No. 7

8 ounces (200 g) plain flour
2 ounces (50 g) sugar
2 teaspoons baking powder
$\frac{1}{2}$ teaspoon salt
1 egg
1 teacup milk
2 ounces (50 g) melted
    butter or margarine

$\frac{1}{2}$ cup blueberries, bilberries
    or blackberries. (Defrosted
    frozen berries can be used
    out of season or $\frac{1}{2}$ a tin of
    blackcurrants, drained.)

Turn on the oven. Butter a bun tin, or you could use the paper cases that fairy cakes are baked in. Sift the flour, sugar, baking powder and salt into a bowl. Beat the egg in another bowl, add the milk and the melted butter and mix well. Add the cleaned fruit to the flour and mix in. Make a well in the centre of the flour and pour in the egg mixture. Mix with a wooden spoon as if you were making a pancake batter, that is, slowly stir the flour from the side into the liquid in the middle. Do this lightly, just until the dry ingredients are moistened. Fill the sections of the bun tin or each paper case about two-thirds full. Place in the oven and cook for 20–25 minutes until the muffins are puffed up and golden brown.

SOUTH AMERICA and The CARIBBEAN

Chilli con Carne
Huevos Rancheros
Papas Chorreadas
Chocolate en Leche
Banana Bread

Mexico has also been squeezed into this section as although that is not strictly correct many of the ingredients, particularly chillis, tomatoes (red and green), corn and corn meal are typical of the whole continent of South America. And though Chilli con Carne is not really typically Mexican, it is so good and popular, it seems a shame to leave it out! In South America itself, many of the countries developed quite separate cooking styles due to their boundaries of mountain ranges and different indigenous Indian tribes and various conquerors and settlers. In its pure form South American cooking has an ancient history. As long ago as 2500 B.C. the Incas of Peru were practising very sophisticated agriculture. They produced many varieties of potato and even developed a form of freeze-drying to preserve them. The Incas, who were sun-worshippers, discovered plants and herbs that lent a yellow (sunny) colour to food and they are still used today. It is hard to summarize South American food. It is a curious mixture of the ancient and the modern, and the really authentic dishes do not travel far from their countries of origin. Of course, steaks are typical of Argentina and Venezuela and much grilled meat is eaten in Brazil. In Chile and Uruguay more fish is eaten, but the predominant flavours of the continent are tomatoes, dried beans, chillis, avocados, cassava, potatoes, corn meal, plantains (green bananas), limes and nuts. The islands of the Caribbean, which Christopher Columbus described as Paradise, have a similarly mixed cuisine, added to and flavoured by the cooking habits of most of the countries of the world. It is robust, spicy, sunny holiday food.

Chilli con Carne

Strictly speaking this dish is probably more authentic to Texas than any points south, but it is so popular and relatively easy, it is worth including. A packet or a tin of *tortillas*, a South American flat bread now available in some large supermarkets and delicatessens, served with it would make *tacos*, which are at least Mexican! Go easy on the chilli powder if you don't like food too peppery, but if you leave it out altogether you will just have stew.

2 tablespoons cooking fat or cooking oil

1½ pounds (600 g) braising steak cut into small cubes (this is better than mince, though you could use mince)

1 large onion chopped

1 clove garlic chopped

1 dessertspoon tomato purée or ketchup

1 teaspoon dried or fresh herbs (oregano is good)

1 teaspoon ground cumin (if you have it)

1 beef stock cube

Chilli powder or chilli sauce

1 teaspoon salt

Trim any fat off the beef and cut it into small cubes the size of a dice. Heat the fat or oil in a heavy frying-pan and fry the meat until it is brown on all sides. Remove the meat with a slotted spoon and add the chopped onion and garlic and cook until they are softened. Mix in the tomato purée, the herbs, salt and chilli (a

teaspoon of powder or bottled sauce is enough to begin with).
Make up the stock cube by mixing it with ¾ pint boiling water
and when it has dissolved pour the stock into the pan. When the
liquid comes to the boil return the meat, lower the heat, and
simmer covered for about 2 hours or until the meat is tender.
Halfway through the cooking, taste to see if you want to hot it up
with more chilli. Chilli con Carne is good served with red kidney
beans or rice or both. You can get red kidney beans in a tin or
cook them from dried following the bean instructions in the
Boston Baked Bean recipe, page 91. To make Tacos, heat the
tortillas according to the instructions on the packet or tin and
serve them wrapped around the meat mixture.

Huevos Rancheros

This means eggs as they are served on the ranch and they would
make such a hearty start to the day, they are probably better for
lunch! Serrano chillies are quite easy to find in cans but half a
green pepper could stand in.

4 eggs

1 ounce (25 g) butter,
margarine or oil

Sauce:

1 tablespoon vegetable oil
2 medium onions finely
chopped
1 medium-size can of peeled
tomatoes

2 serrano chillies from a tin *or*
½ green pepper
2 pinches of sugar
A pinch of salt and pepper

Heat the oil in a saucepan and fry the onions, stirring them
around until they are soft but not brown. If you are using green
pepper, chop it finely, making sure it is free from seeds, add it to
the pan and cook for a few minutes. Add the tinned tomatoes,
the serrano chillies, drained and finely chopped, and the sugar,
salt and pepper. Simmer uncovered for about 15 minutes or until
the sauce is quite thick. In a frying-pan, fry the eggs in the butter
or oil and when they are ready, serve each one on a plate surrounded with the tomato sauce. To make a more substantial
meal, you could serve the egg on half a crisp roll or a slice of
toast.

Papas Chorreadas

Papas, meaning potatoes, along with tomatoes, are two ingredients that came to our part of the world from South America only a relatively short time ago. The Inca and pre-Incaic people, who were gifted botanists, developed over a hundred varieties of potato as early as 2500 B.C. This dish combines both discoveries in a particularly delicious manner.

1 pound (400 g) potatoes
2 ounces (50 g) butter, lard, margarine or cooking oil
1 onion
1 small can of tomatoes
2 tablespoons double cream

4 ounces (100 g) grated mild cheese (a mild Cheddar or Lancashire or Caerphilly)
Salt and pepper
A pinch of ground cumin (optional)

Scrub the potatoes and boil them in salted water until they are tender. Drain them and when they are cool enough, peel off the skins and keep the potatoes warm in a low oven. Peel and chop the onion. Melt the butter in a frying-pan and fry the onion until it is softened but not brown. Drain the tomatoes from their can, add them with a pinch of salt, pepper and cumin, if you are using it. Simmer for about 5 minutes until the tomatoes have broken up and formed a sauce. Add the cream, stir, then drop in the grated cheese in small handfuls stirring all the while. Don't let the mixture boil. When the cheese is all melted, pour the sauce over the potatoes and serve.

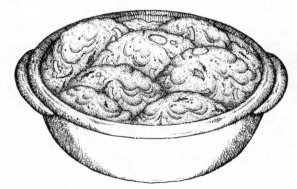

Chocolate en Leche

Hot chocolate was probably drunk by the Aztecs and is therefore, quite rightly, a Royal drink. Use a plain darker chocolate for the right Mexican flavour and whip up as much froth as possible. A blender could help you here.

4 ounces (100 g) plain
  chocolate
1 pint (6 dl) milk

½ teaspoon ground cinnamon
A drop or two of almond
  essence (optional)

Break the chocolate into squares and put in a saucepan with the milk. Cook over a very low heat stirring all the time until the chocolate has completely melted and blended with the milk. Let the milk get very hot, but not boiling. Add the cinnamon and almond essence, if you are using it. Take the pan off the stove and with an egg-beater whisk the mixture until it is frothy. Pour it into cups and serve.

Banana Bread

Bananas play a big part in sunny Caribbean cookery. Called Plantains they are often cooked while still green and occur in every course from soups to desserts. This Banana Bread from Jamaica is lovely at tea-time, buttered or plain, and it is a good way of using up over-ripe bananas.

Oven time : 1 hour
Oven setting : electric 350°F, gas No. 4

4 ounces (100 g) butter or
  margarine
4 ounces (100 g) sugar
1 egg
8 ounces (200 g) plain flour
1 dessertspoon baking powder
2 large very ripe bananas

2 ounces (50 g) seedless
  raisins
2 ounces (50 g) chopped
  walnuts
A pinch of salt
A pinch of nutmeg

Cream the butter and sugar together in a bowl until they are light and fluffy. This is hard to do if the butter is chilled. Cut it into small squares and leave it at room temperature for about an hour if that is the problem. Add the egg and beat again. Sift the flour, baking powder, salt and nutmeg into another bowl. Peel the bananas and mash them with a fork. Add the dry ingredients and the bananas alternately to the creamed butter, beating after each addition. Add the raisins and nuts and mix well. Pour the mixture into a loaf tin and bake in the oven for 1 hour or until a skewer poked in comes out clean. Cool on a cake rack and serve in slices.

NEW ZEALAND and AUSTRALIA

Kangaroo Tail Soup
Barbecues
Dampers and Billy Tea
New Zealand Lamb with
    New Zealand Honey
Pavlova

There are not a lot of dishes that are typically Australian or associated only with New Zealand. Food in these countries tends to be simple, made from good home-grown ingredients and lots of it. Because of the favourable climate, barbecues play a large part in family life, social life, and beach life. Barbecues needn't only mean grilled meat. You can cook fruit and vegetables on the open fire and the difference in flavour is as good as the difference between charcoal grilled meat and that cooked in a gas or electric oven. The first Australian 'barbecues' were the bushmen's camp fire cookery, of which the two most famous elements are dampers and billy tea. The Aborigines of Australia long ago discovered what we might call cooking in an oven brick. They would wrap their meat, which could be snakes or lizards, in damp clay, and cook it in the embers of a fire. The Maoris of New Zealand make an oven out of a hole in the ground covered with a fire, and often prepare feasts that way. Fruit which grows so well in these countries is often mixed with meat in various stews and is the filling for the dessert that seems for ever Australian – a Pavlova cake. Steak for breakfast or a hearty lamb dinner would put you in the right frame of mind to tackle the food of this huge continent.

Kangaroo Tail Soup

Since kangaroo is in short supply at most butchers outside
Australia, an ox-tail can be used instead. It makes a very rich,
tasty broth, good enough to make you jump with joy!

2 pounds (1 kg) ox-tail,
  jointed into sections
2 tablespoons beef dripping
2 onions
2 carrots

2 sticks of celery
2 beef stock cubes
2 bay leaves
A pinch of ground nutmeg
Salt and pepper

While you are preparing the vegetables, soak the ox-tail seg-
ments (trimmed of any large pieces of fat) in cold salted water.
Peel and slice the onions and carrots and clean and chop the
celery. Melt the fat in a large pan and fry the vegetables until
they are lightly browned. Drain and dry the ox-tail pieces and
add them to the pan and brown them. Make up the beef stock
cubes with 2 pints (1·2 litres) of water and add the stock, plus the
bay leaves, nutmeg, and two pinches salt and pepper. Add
another 1½ pints (9 dl) of water. Bring to the boil, then turn the
heat down low so the soup just simmers with the lid on the pan.
Leave it to simmer for about 2½ hours when the meat will be
coming away from the bones. Ask someone to help you strain
the soup into another pan. When the bones have cooled, take the
meat off them and add it to the soup. Taste to see if you need
more salt and pepper and make very hot again.

Barbecues

Reliably sunny weather makes barbecues the most popular way
of cooking and entertaining in Australia and New Zealand. There
are no real recipes for a barbecue, just a general rule; almost
anything tastes better cooked outside over an open fire.

Wrapping items in foil seems to me to miss the whole point of a barbecue (since it seals out the charcoal or woody flavour) and much tastier results come from leaving meat in one of the mixtures given below (that is called marinating) and brushing it with the marinade while it is cooking. Sausages, chops, steaks, hamburgers, frankfurters, kebabs, chicken pieces are some of the obvious ingredients for a barbecue. But don't forget vegetables which can be brushed with oil and cooked straight on the grid. Carrot slices, large onion rings, sections of green pepper, slices of aubergine, whole courgettes, are wonderful done this way. Or thread them on skewers with or without cubes of meat.

BASIC MARINADE

This is ideal for pieces of beef or lamb for kebabs, or for chops.

1 cup of cooking oil
The juice of 1 lemon
or 1 tablespoon wine vinegar

1 clove garlic, crushed
A pinch of salt and pepper
Some herbs of your choice

Mix everything together in a bowl and put the meat in. Turn it occasionally. You can leave it a few hours or overnight in the fridge or a cool spot.

ORIENTAL MARINADE

This is very good with chicken or pork fillet or slices of beef.

1 cup vegetable oil
2 tablespoons soya sauce
1 tablespoon vinegar
1 clove garlic, crushed

A pinch of ginger
A small piece of orange or
tangerine rind

Mix together and pour over the meat. Leave the meat in the liquid for a few hours and then, wearing oven gloves, brush the meat with the mixture while it is cooking.

IRANIAN MARINADE

Delicious with lamb or chicken

2 small cartons of plain
yogurt

A pinch of thyme

Mix the yogurt and thyme and cover the meat and leave for 12–24 hours in a cool place. Grill the meat with the yogurt still clinging to it.

Dampers and Billy Tea

Once a jolly swagman, waiting till his billy boiled, sang 'Who'll Come A-Waltzing Matilda With Me?' Perhaps the most typical Australian meal would be a campfire one, and Dampers (the bushman's bread), are the right accompaniment to any meat or stew you might be cooking. You *could* cook them in the oven but they would be nothing without that taste of woodsmoke.

DAMPERS

8 ounces (200 g) of plain flour	1 teaspoon salt
1 tablespoon baking powder	Water

Mix the flour, baking powder, salt and gradually add water until you have a stiff dough. Knead it together until it is smooth. Roll pieces of it into long sausage shapes. Peel the bark from a stick, preferably a green one that won't easily burn, or soak an older stick. Wind the damper dough around the stick and cook it in the hot embers of the fire or on top of a barbecue. When the dough is cooked, slide it off the stick and maybe slide in a cooked sausage or fried bacon. Dampers are good eaten with jam or golden syrup too.

BILLY TEA

To make billy tea, you put a handful of tea leaves into a billy can (or kettle) of boiling water. The billy is then boiled for as long as it takes to round up the sheep (one minute is ideal!). Strain it into mugs and drink with milk and sugar. It is a strong, powerful brew.

New Zealand Lamb with New Zealand Honey

Lamb is understandably the favourite meat of most New Zealanders. Lamb chops, which can be a bit boring if grilled quite plain, are transformed with the honey and mustard into a dish of distinction. Don't be put off by thinking you don't like mustard. The sweetness of the honey will calm down its 'hotness'.

4 lamb chops (or a packet of thin 'breakfast' chops as sold in supermarkets)

1 tablespoon honey
2 teaspoons French mustard
Salt and pepper

Turn on the grill to medium high. Mix the honey and mustard in a bowl with a pinch of salt and two pinches of pepper. Spread one side of each chop thinly with the mixture. Grill for a few minutes (if thin chops) or longer for chunky ones. Using oven gloves, remove the chops from the grill, spread the uncooked side with the honey and mustard and grill again.

Pavlova

This light as air meringue dessert was named to honour the visit to Australia of that light-as-air dancer, Anna Pavlova. When cooked, it should have a slightly gooey, chewy, centre inside a crisp crust. Any fruit, or mixture of fruit, or well-drained tinned fruit is good on top of this cake.

3 egg whites
6 ounces (150 g) castor sugar
1 teaspoon cornflour
1 teaspoon vinegar

A pinch of salt
Slices of fresh fruit or a mixture of fruits or drained, tinned fruit
1 carton whipping cream

Oven time : $1\frac{1}{2}$ hours
Oven setting : electric 250°F, gas No. $\frac{1}{2}$

Turn on the oven. Line the bottom of a 7-inch (175-mm) cake tin with a circle of foil. Use a piece of kitchen paper to rub a drop of cooking oil all over the foil. In a large, spotlessly clean mixing bowl, beat the egg whites with a rotary beater until they are foamy. Add the salt and beat some more until the whites are stiff and hold their own shape. Add the sugar in four lots, beating after each addition. When the mixture is shiny and standing in peaks, mix the cornflour and vinegar together and fold it into the meringue. Do this with a metal spoon and as lightly as possible so as not to lose the airiness of the meringue. Spoon the meringue into the tin and spread it to cover the base, making the edges a little higher than the centre. Place in the oven. After the time is up, remove the tin, using oven gloves, and let the meringue cool in the tin. Carefully turn it out and gently peel the foil away. Place the Pavlova on a plate, pile on your chosen fruit and cover with the cream which you have whipped until thick but not stiff. Serve immediately.

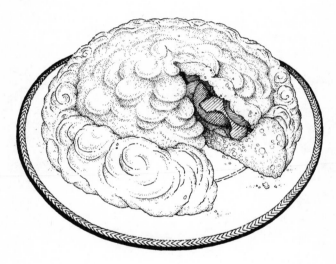

Index